STOP Predators COLD!
Series

How To Protect Your Child From Sexual Predators

Preston Jones and Joyce Jackson
Keeping Kids Safe
Copyright 2007

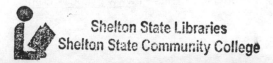

Keeping Kids Safe
903 Monet Circle
Walnut Creek, CA 94597

Get Two Additional FREE Gifts At
www.pycbook.com

"If you want extra protection for your child from sexual predators, visit this website!..."

Plus 3 More SECRETS You'll Read About In The Letter On That Site...

Now YOU Can Get Every Secret We've Created!...

PLUS 5 Amazing *Additional* FREE Bonus Gifts!...

www.pycbook.com

TABLE OF CONTENTS

Enormity Of The Problem…Basic Fears To Face…It Could Happen To You…Dangers Of False Ideas…Extreme Predators

The Ultimate Safety Secret….Improve This And Your Child Will Be Safer… …Defining Ultimate Safety… The Philosophy Of Safety… Setting The Example

Where Real Safety Begins…Changing Your Destiny For Your Child…The Proven Success Formula For Safe Kids…Serious Fun For Safer Kids

The Sly Disguises Of Online Sexual Predators…The Warning Signs You Must Know That Your Child Is In Danger From An Online Predator…The Dangers Of Social Networks And Blogs…The 10 Secrets For Internet Safety Today

Five Proven Safety Secrets For Playing Outside…Extra Security In Neighborhood

WHAT READERS SAY
ABOUT THIS BOOK

"After just 5 seconds browsing the Table of Contents I KNEW I needed to get this book for my sister to use with my niece and nephew. This book is full of so many priceless gems I predict it will not only be a HUGE best-seller, but will also save thousands of children from sexual predators."

- Jason Oman,
#1 International Best-Selling Author of 'Conversations with Millionaires'
www.JasonOman.com

One idea alone from Preston Jones' and Joyce Jackson's "How To Protect Your Child From Sexual Predators" can make a difference in the world!

Here's Why...
Their Safe ideas are bar-none, no questions asked absolutely, the best-of-the-best ideas for keeping kids safe!

Do Not take this lightly Their ideas are a *Life Saving*.
- John Di Lemme
Strategic Business Coach
International Motivational Speaker
www.FindYourWhy.com
(Alexa Ranking in the teens)

Parents

I feel like I can finally do something to protect my children. I am not powerless against predators any more!
- Sandra Jones – Walnut Creek, CA

This book is really good! The tips are things I can do immediately and see results in my kids. I feel that my kids can really be safer today.

Grandparents

"Preston and Joyce are on a mission. They have a passion for keeping YOUR children safe from predators. If you have a child, grandchild, niece or nephew, (or you know someone who does) you NEED this book.

Joyce taught my grandchildren some simple safety tips. Just a few days later, my 8 year old grandson was approached in a public playground at an amusement park by a bad stranger. The "Belly Brain" that Joyce taught him kicked in. He knew exactly what to do, and he walked away from what could have been a very dangerous situation. Joyce, I can't thank you enough."
- Frank Sousa
www.trafficgeyser.com
www.coolwebtips.com

INTRODUCTION

STOP Sexual Predators COLD!

We're going to show you how to protect your child from sexual predators. Our approach to child safety along with our effective techniques will enable you to STOP Sexual Predators COLD!

We believe every child deserves the right to grow up safe. Every child deserves this right by birth. They deserve it no matter where they live, who they are or what their background or circumstances dictate.

We believe this right so strongly that we have dedicated most of our lives and business to making sure this can be a reality for all kids.

Children are to be nurtured and offered the right to be the best they can be as human beings. As a collective group, they are our future. They are the future of the human race. All of us have a stake in making sure children are safe and secure and grow up to reach their full potential as human beings. Sexual predators, in fact, any people that use and abuse children in anyway, are vermin that must be stopped. Abuse ruins lives. Abuse tears apart families. Abuse devastates the child victim and their self image.

Adults who were victims of sexual predators as children can spend a lifetime healing from the damage forced upon them. Sexual predators negatively affect the course of people's lives and it is wrong and especially unfair to innocent children. There is also no such thing as an "isolated" abuse of a child incident. Abuse does not happen and then magically stop and "go away." Abuse takes time and effort to heal and it is the victim and their families that suffer.

We are leveling the playing field, so to speak. We are out to help kids and parents stop the criminals. We also go one step further and teach kids to keep themselves safe. We show kids and their families how to thwart sexual predators cold in their tracks. We'll help you stay in front of the problem.

And, the problem cannot be overstated. According to a study released in 2002 by the National Incidence Studies of Missing, Abducted, Runaway, and Thrown-away Children (NISMART II), an estimated 6 children per hour are abducted by a non-family member. In approximately 50% of these cases, the children are sexually assaulted. By the time children are 18, the surveys indicate that as many as one in eight boys and one in five girls will have been sexually abused.

This makes every child a potential target for sexual predators. This could make your child an unwitting target, too. Don't let that happen!

Every parent today has to worry about keeping their child safe from sexual predators. This is where we help. This is where we will arm you with the tips, information, techniques and the "know-how" behind them, to keep your child safer today than yesterday. We will show you how to teach your child to keep themselves safe from sexual predators, too.

Sexual predators are on our streets, in our neighborhoods and at our schools. Not only are they there, they are an ever growing danger on the Internet.
Be prepared and take charge of you child's safety. Threats are everywhere in today's dangerous world. They all must be stopped. Our kids must be safe. You can do it with this book.

We established and developed Keeping Kids Safe for this very reason. Our purpose is to keep kids safe by teaching them to KEEP THEMSELVES SAFE. By teaching the kids to keep themselves safe we add an extra layer of safety and protection to every child.

Any child is safe when Mom and Dad are around. Kids come to rely on Mom and Dad to do just that. But toddlers go to preschool and preschoolers go to elementary school and elementary school kids go to middle school and middle school kids hang out at malls among other places. Kids will be out and about on their own as much as if not more, without their parents.

The point here is, there are plenty of opportunities for predators to assault your child when you are not around. So we at Keeping Kids Safe are going to help. We're going to help by reinforcing many of the things parents do well at home. We may even teach you a little bit you didn't know, too.

Who wouldn't want to sleep just a little better at night knowing their child is just a little safer? We are here to keep kids safe, all kids. Sometimes, we even help make better families in the process.

Our unique approach to child safety folds the entire family into the safety process. We work with the kids, then fold in the parents and when we have their attention, we can teach both of them some very effective safety techniques. We wouldn't have it any other way.

It is fun and exciting for the children in our classes and even fun for the parents that bring them. We teach a subject as serious as personal safety in a fun and fun-filled manner. The bottom line is, our ideas and techniques have to be reinforced at home which means families need to embrace our ideas to be the safest they can be.

Another reason our approach is so effective is that at Keeping Kids Safe, we focus on staying one step in front of the predators. We focus on solutions for safe kids and preventing situations that could cause kids to be pulled in, surprised, trapped and abducted.

The solution starts with us and takes hold with you, the parents.
We will continue our work because of our vision of all children owning the right to grow up safe. It continues to propel us forward to offer our child safety program to wider and wider audiences.

We never assume to leave a child's safety in today's dangerous world to chance. Never assume an assault on you child could never happen to you.

Take charge and control of your child's safety right now! Make sure your kids know you are in charge of it, too. While most kid's reactions are negative to more parental control, they subconsciously need guidance from you. They need to know their safety matters to you, so tell them and show them it does.

It's all about the kids. We are all here for the kids and their right to grow up safe in today's world.

This book provides our effective tips and techniques for preventing sexual predators from abusing any more kids. For the criminal on the street or online, we're putting them on notice that they are out of business.

How This Book Can Help You

This book provides our effective tips and techniques for preventing sexual predators from abusing any more kids, your kids. For the criminal on the street or online, we're putting them on notice that they are out of business.

Flip through the book and pick a chapter that appeals to you. Read it. Then find another.

The book is intended to be used as a reference guide for you whenever you need it. Each chapter is written to stand on its own. Read a section that appeals to you, apply it's information and come back for more information later.

It's all about your kids. It's all about keeping them safe for their entire lifetime.

1

THE MAGIC FORMULA FOR KEEPING KIDS SAFE

Owning The Power To Keep Your Child Safe

Parents! Your child's safety from sexual predators depends on you!

Not a bad opening for a book on child safety. Now that we have your attention, it is true. We teach kids to keep themselves safe. We also teach kids to be responsible for themselves, too. The most important thing, however, the crucial piece, in making it work, are you, the parents, taking the responsibility for insuring it is all put into place.

You must own the responsibility for keeping your child safe. You must make sure they learn how to keep themselves safe from sexual predators when you are not around.

Anytime you go out and about with your child they are pretty safe with you. You hold their hands, talk to them and make sure your family group stays together as you scour the mall, trot through the zoo or head to your table at the restaurant.

What happens when your child is playing in the yard when you're inside, at school, walking the dog or walking home from the store, is what really matters. Your child must have the ability to keep themselves safe in today's world prowled by sexual predators, when you are not around. And, Mom and Dad, it is your responsibility to make sure they have this "keep themselves safe" ability.

Easily said by glib safety experts, but what does this really mean? More importantly, how do you do this from a simple little book?

To be honest, it is pretty simple. It means you must stand up and grab hold of an incredible power waiting for you to command and control. It is called the "Power To Keep Your Child Safe." Sometimes we call it mentoring.

Mentoring your child goes beyond parenting. It gets into making a positive difference by influencing your child to be the best they can be as a person. Mentoring means you maximize your commitment. It means doing what needs to be done. It means when you're tired, sick or fed up you still take the time and patience to insure your child is safe for their entire lifetime. Being responsible means teaching your child to be safe in a constant and consistent series of small steps everyday.

Is it easy to do? That depends on you. What is your commitment to your child? What is your commitment to your child's safety?

If you answered resoundingly, "100%!" then it will be easy for you. You're reading this book because you are already a mentor to your child. Your child's safety for an entire lifetime can be simple and easy with a few tips to added to the mentoring skills you already possess.

If you have not gone beyond basic parenting then we'll help you make the jump into true mentoring. It is one thing to understand responsibility. It is another to own it. Owning it is harnessing its power. Simply put, you own your child's safety. You make it work. Show and guide your child every step of the way in what to do and how to do it. Own the responsibility in making sure they understand it and learn it. Help them learn for a lifetime how to keep themselves safe from sexual predators when you are not around.

The Word That Work Miracles

"Commitment" is a word that, as an adult, you no doubt have seen and heard throughout your lifetime. It is over-used, we hear it too much and can easily tune it out.

Be careful!

"Commitment" is a very powerful word that can work miracles. It is only overused by those that chose to ignore it. You should pay attention to this word and its meaning, especially when it comes to your child's safety.

If you worry about sexual predators, now is the time to pay attention to this word "Commitment" with new interest and resolve.

Few things are as powerful to you as commitment. Commitment can miraculously turn ordinary, sometimes less than ordinary, individuals into leaders, dream achievers and successful human beings.

You must commit to your child's safety. We have to ask:

"As a parent, are you truly committed to your child's safety?"

Of course, everyone reading this book will say, "Yes!" But there is a follow up question, and that is:
"How much time will you spend each day doing the techniques and exercises we have in this book, with your child?"

Your answer to this question is a measure of your commitment. Time is a precious commodity for anyone, especially a parent, in today's fast-paced world. Time, however, is required for commitment. There is no way around it.

The Keeping Kids Safe techniques and suggestions we provide take 5 to 10 minutes each day. That's all. Are you committed to that? How important is your child's safety from sexual predators?

It is actually easier than that. If you understand what we are saying, if you embrace our philosophy of child safety, then the techniques are integrated into what you are already doing as a committed parent, not adding any more time a day to your already crazy schedule.

In the worst case, if the Keeping Kids Safe Safety techniques added 30 or 60 minutes a day to your busy schedule, would your commitment still be there? Again, what price is your child's safety from sexual predators?

We are just making a point, here. We have intentionally made he information in the book readily available to you and easy to follow and use, in minutes a day. You just need to commit to use it.

We hope your commitment is a resounding "Yes!" to your child's safety. Our methods do not require hours a day or even 30 minutes a day. However, the commitment is still required. "Required" is a harsh word when preceded by the word "commitment."

We have a saying with the kids in our classes, "Too Bad, So Sad!" and we'll use it here.   Five minutes a day or fifteen minutes every-other-day is reasonable for your child's lifelong safety. As a parent, you must simply be accountable for providing the impetus and commitment to achieving true safety for your children. We just make it simple for you.

Committing to your child's safety needs to be viewed as a sacred vow. We are challenging you now to read every word of this book. We are challenging you to follow through on just 10% of what you read here. Can you do it?

View your commitment as the foundation of a lifetime of safety for your child. We believe commitment is the foundation to your child's safety success. Make the foundation strong, make it solid.

With a solid commitment from you, your child will see how serious you are about their safety. They will then take it more seriously themselves. It's called "leading by example," another important step in committing to your child's safety.

If you do, you will help your child be safe from sexual predators and be safer today then they were yesterday.

The Power of Clarity

What will commitment do for you as a parent? What will it do for your child's safety?

The answer is simple: it will give you the Power of Clarity. It will give you a targeted purpose to focus on and a goal to head towards. You can move forward with a laser focused purpose of keeping your child safe from sexual predators.

Clarity of focus and vision is powerful.

Clarity, power of vision and focus, are very good things to possess as a parent. It means you filter through the maze of everything constantly being thrown at you and zero in on the things that are truly important for your child, like their safety.

Clarity of your goal for safety will come with making a commitment to your child's safety program. The importance of this goes beyond the obvious safety benefits for your child. The importance of clarity benefits you directly, especially when you need to maintain your commitment.

We all go through up and downs in life. What distinguishes one individual from another however, is their commitment to a clear purpose, a goal. It is called goal setting. Commitment. Clarity. Goals. They go hand in hand. So does achieving that goal.

Committing to your child's safety is pretty easy. So is getting started with it.

Maintaining it can be a trick. Being human, we all go through times when our resolve can weaken. Find ways to strengthen your resolve.

For example, when your commitment to your child's safety waivers, re-read this book. Read other inspirational books. Talk to other like-minded parents about their commitment to their children. Find positive motivation in CD's you can pop into your radio or your car. The solutions are endless, but keep your commitment to keeping sexual predators at bay and your child safe, fresh and real every day.

Also, keep your approach simple. The simpler the better. Clarity comes with simplicity. Keep your approach to your child's safety simple and easy for your lifestyle. When you struggle with your time, when it seems like your kids are endlessly crabby, when it seems like you just want to give up, the best thing to do to keep your commitment alive is clear away everything to its simplest form. Go back to basics. Make everything simple. Refresh yourself. And, most of all persevere.

We are here for you. We work with families and parents, too. Safe kids mean great families with parents committed to a lifetime of safety.

If you are truly committed to your child's safety, then you are truly ready to learn and implement real safety techniques starting with our 5 Secrets Of Safe Kids.

The 5 Secrets Of Safe Kids

There are 5 Secrets we have learned that truly make kids safe. These Secrets set the foundation of true safety for a lifetime in children, and can do the same for your child.

These Secrets will also surprise you. They work quietly and effectively beneath the surface of your child's brain. If you use these 5 Secrets, they will make any safety technique that much more effective. Without these 5 Secrets, your child will never be able to keep themselves safe. Ever.

Secret #1: Confidence
Confidence and a positive self image are crucial in good child safety. Confident kids are less of a target for sexual predators. Not only do they stand taller and keep their heads up higher, they represent a problem, a less than easy victim for sexual predators.

Confident kids project "struggle" for any predator trolling for kids and more often than not, predators will pass them by. More often, predators will choose kids that appear weak and sad, a child in need of a friend. These are the kids that hang their heads, shuffle down the street and have a hard time looking anyone in the eye when they talk to them.

Confidence is a powerful deterrent.
And yet, there is something more, something deeper when your child is confident. We notice confident kids display certain structural changes, physical changes in their bodies that serve them better than kids that

have poor self-images. Confident kids can control their physical movements a little bit better. At the same time, they can move more quickly and with finer control of those movements. We find confident kids can actually focus better mentally and for longer periods of time.

In other words, these kids are better equipped physically, mentally and emotionally to learn the actual safety techniques that could save them from sexual predators than kids that feel bad about themselves. Kids that hang their head, shuffle around, are tired or ill, cannot move with as much control or quickness or think as clearly as kids that are healthy and confident. A high degree of self confidence and a positive self image matter in good child safety.

Secret #2: Empowerment
Empowering your child to take care of themselves is one of the most powerful Safety Secret we can offer you.

When you empower your child, you truly teach them to make choices for themselves. When you mentor them as a parent you actually guide them into learning to make good, positive choices for themselves on their own. When they can do this, they will truly be safe for a lifetime.

In its simplest form, empowerment means

your child feels like they have a measure of control over their life. They feel they can make their own decisions. Most kids don't feel this ability. Most kids do not have it, either. Parents and adults are constantly making decisions for children:

- When to eat
- What to eat
- When to get up
- When to go to sleep
- Where to go
- Who to go with
- What to do

The list can go on endlessly. Life for a child can feel completely out of their control. Kids will engage in a struggle with their parents to get some control of their lives. In doing so it usually comes across as conflict.

- No! I don't want to go!
- I don't like that!
- I'm not eating that!
- Stop it!
- I don't want to!
- Leave me alone!

The Secret to empowering your child, even at the youngest of ages, is in giving them their own choices to make. Give them alternatives to situations in their lives, let them make some of their own choices.

This too, can be pretty simple. For example,

instead of serving them broccoli, ask them to choose between carrots, peas or broccoli or another vegetable. Give them a choice to make instead of just putting one on their plate. Instead of the green dress, ask your daughter which one she would like to wear. Instead of forcing your child into the brown shoes, ask them which ones they would like to put on today.

These are pretty simple examples, but this about as easy as it gets in empowering your child. Giving your child choices is crucial in their development. It is crucial in their ability to keep themselves safe, too.

Making choices matters to kids. When you do this simple, easy thing, miracles will happen within them. An empowered child starts to feel good about themselves. And what would consistent, good feelings about themselves lead to? Confidence!

Will your child always make good choices for themselves? No. That is where you, Mom and Dad, come into the picture. You, as a mentor to your child, can guide them through the array of choices they will face. You can guide them and teach them about good choices and the benefits of making good choices for themselves. It is what safe kids are all about.

Secret #3: Catch Them Being Good
When your child makes a bad choice, it's

important for you to stay calm about it. Yes, this is easier said then done. However, it is critical in your child's ability to keep themselves safe, that you learn to take their mistakes in stride.

We want you to spend more time and energy catching your child being good.

A subtle prodding towards better choices is more effective than highlighting, in a big emotional way, any bad choice they make for themselves. If you have to highlight negative behavior, be very careful in saying, "That was a bad choice," rather than "You are bad." Take care to say, "You can make better choices," instead of saying, "How stupid!" Things like, "You're a great kid but that choice could have been better," keeps your child's image of themselves solid and highlights the choice only, not them, as being bad. Your child is good, the choice is bad.

Building confidence, building a solid self image in your child, builds safety. Capitalize on this and highlight the good things they do more often than the bad things. As a matter of fact, focus on highlighting as many good things as you can rather than making a big deal about the bad things they may do.

We call it, "Catch Them Being Good."

We think positive reinforcement is a much stronger teaching tool and technique for child safety than negative reinforcement.

Praise your child when you see them doing good behaviors. Lavish the praise and adulation onto them when they do really great things. This is also positive mentoring. This is channeling your child into learning how to make good, solid and positive choices for themselves. It builds and fosters that ever-so-critical confidence in themselves.

It is easier to notice the bad behavior. We are tuned by society to notice the negative and bad things people do. It is very easy to notice the bad things your child does. It is a focus of many parents, naturally. Reverse the trend and make your focal point the things your child does well. Positive reinforcement will teach your child to repeat those behaviors you want and make it easier for you to guide them into those good choices.

Secret #4: Listening
Another crucial Secret in teaching kids to be safe is to let them know you are listening to them.

Listening to your child goes beyond the standard, "Yep. Un huh. Sure." These kinds of responses they get daily. True listening, the kind that allows your child to feel like they are really being heard and understood, is a special parenting skill.

Listening to your child happens in two ways: one, you allow them to say what they need to say, in their words, in their way, however they want to say it. It may be challenging to follow this advice, especially when your child speaks in disjointed sentences or jumbled words. They may take 5 or 10 minutes out of your busy day, but just let them talk without interrupting them. You can tell when it is important versus when they are just mumbling or making noise. Sit and listen to them. Take the time, make the time.

Two, listen to what they say without judgment. Even if you do not like what you hear, even if you feel upset by what you hear, listen to it. Be quiet, look them in the eyes with your full attention and simply listen to them.

Your child is coming to you. They need your attention. They believe at that moment you will listen to them. Do it. Reserve judgment and negative feelings about what they are saying for another time.

When you do this you are building on the future, on your child's safety. They need to feel, deep inside, they can tell you about anything. They need the security of knowing you will listen to them and what they have to say. If your child is threatened in any way, they will need to come to you, Mom or Dad, and tell you. That rapport and comfort for them needs to be established at a young age. You start by simply listening to them.

Secret #5: Repetition

This last Secret is probably the most important of all. We can teach your kids in the classroom. We can put all of our information into a book for you to read. However, it is all useless unless you use it and apply it, day in and day out at home.

In our classroom we work with kids 45 minutes at a time, once a week. You may read this book 10 minutes a day until you finish it.
True learning for your child comes with repetition. That is your job. You need to do it at home.

Repetition does not need to be boring, either. Make games out of things you want to teach. Use fun words and phrases your child uses when talking about safety. Fold in your child's favorite toys, cartoon characters or things they like into activities you do several times a week. These are simple yet exciting skills for reinforcement activities. It's repetition with excitement. What a great way to learn for any child!

Working with our techniques is also something to do a few times a week. Stay away from daily practice routines as if this was a sport as this is the surest way to bore your child and lose their attention.

Make learning safety fun. Make it exciting. Fold in the whole family and enjoy learning about true safety for a lifetime together.

I Will Always Do My Best

We start our 10 week safety program classes, and every class in the series, with the Keeping Kids Safe "2 Cardinal Rules" for the kids:

- I Will Always Do My Best!

- I Will Always Say I Can!

These Rules are very simple, easy ideas, yet they contain great depth and effectiveness for your child's safety from sexual predators. First, we've mentioned that if your child is confident, they are less of a target for sexual predators. It goes even further than that. If your child can even create an appearance of being confident, happy, strong and healthy, when you are not around, they can be less of target for sexual predators.

So what about the kids that are not so confident? This is where learning to appear confident can help. We can teach kids to pretend they are confident. What follows most of the time is that if we can teach a child to pretend they are confident and practice this pretense, they will, over time, actually begin to evolve into a confident child.

Practicing walking with their head up, practicing feeling good, practicing being happy, eventually sinks beneath the surface over time. We actually have a "Feel Good" game we play in our classrooms just for this purpose. Practicing "feeling good" at home, too, with support from their parents, can really begin to set a foundation of confidence in most kids, as well.

Therefore, we really use the 2 Cardinal Rules constantly and right from the start. Confidence in kids is so crucial to their safety that we use these rules all the time to build and build and build some more, onto the foundation of safety we want to set in place.

If we can get kids to verbally recite and say these rules, we can then begin to inject real feeling into how they say them. Pretending you're a confident kid is one thing but adding feelings and emotion into it takes this to a whole other level.

Super Kids And Super Heroes

This other level we take it to is about the kids becoming a Super Hero. Super Heroes are confident and can do anything to a super degree in a child's mind. More than that, Super Heroes are fun for kids. They are fantasy creations kids can relate to very easily and readily. Kids see cartoons with Super Heroes and Super Characters in them. Those characters can do anything. Kids want to do the same things and therefore they have a natural attraction to these characters. We exploit this attraction. We want kids to believe they can be Super heroes, too.

We'll ask the kids who their favorite characters and Super Heroes are. We ask them to tell us why they like them and how they can imitate their favorite Super Hero traits. Whether it's Superman, Luke Skywalker, Arial or Snow White, each one in the end outsmarts "evil." We simply tell kids that their Super Heroes have special "Powers" and it's "OK" for them to have and use some of these "Special Powers," too, like confidence.

It works.

We wind in this idea week in and week out. As classes progress each week we encourage the kids to stand up and tell everyone what they did during the week to be like their Super Hero. After a few weeks most kids start to look forward to getting up in front of the class and telling their story.

At the end of each story we applaud. The applause from the kids and crowd reinforces our positive, self-image building exercises. Approbation, acceptance and encouragement enhance our effort in seeding, growing and building confidence in each child.

When a child relates how they behaved confidently in some way over their past week, we seal it into their mind with "That Was Super!" and "You're Great For Doing That!"

These are very carefully chosen words. These words are about telling each child how great they are. The child is great. We tell them the things they did were super, but they, themselves, are "great." It is just another building block in the foundation of solid self confidence we want to install in each child.

There is a series of Super Hero games we play, too, with the kids that again, fold into learning and building confidence. One is called the "Feel Bad, Feel Good" game. First, we talk to the kids about how their Super Heroes always stand tall, shoulders back, head high and look strong. Then we tell them we want them to look like their

Super Hero and want to play a game with them.

In this game we let the kids walk around the room and at the command of "Feel Bad" they hang their heads, shuffle around and moan. We actually ask them to go back to a time when they might have been sick or sad, and remember what that feels like in their bodies. In doing so, we can actually begin to see some of the children sagging in their posture.

Then we ask them to remember a time when they were really, really happy and excited. Perhaps it was their birthday. Perhaps it was Christmas Day, opening presents. Whatever it is, we take the kids there in their minds for a brief few seconds and here, too, we can see them physically straightening up as they envision their happy, exciting moments.

The start of the game comes with our gentle reminders of both of the feelings. At the command of "Feel Good! Super Hero!" they stand upright, throw their shoulders back, hold their head high and smile as they pop around the room. At the command of "Feel Bad!" they slow down, slink and shuffle around and hang their heads.

Through a series of "Feel Bad!" and "Feel Good! Super Hero!" commands we expose them to the way these two states feel and the bodily sensations that each of them create.

We want them to be able to differentiate between physically feeling good and feeling bad.

More importantly, when we see they understand the difference, we can then teach them to pretend they can "Feel Good" even when they don't. What we are really doing is getting them to turn feeling good on whenever they want to do it. They can project confidence even though they may not feel that way for any number of reasons. We can now get them to "Feel Good" and appear so – meaning appearing more confident – especially when they are outside or alone. We can get kids to appear better and confident even when they don't feel that way so they are less of a target for predators.

Kids can learn to fake out predators with these simple games. They give a child an extra edge of safety whenever they may find themselves alone without Mom or Dad. Its all about staying one step ahead of the sexual predators.

We also find that if kids can begin to feel good when they need to or want to, they tend to like how it feels. They slowly begin to gravitate more and more to those good feelings we show them. It means they can really take hold if parents reinforce these ideas at home.

The games we play merely introduce children to good feelings of confidence. However, we find that kids want to build on them once they experience them. Playing games are simply the first step in an intentional sequence of safety techniques we want the kids to embrace and learn. It all follows a well thought out plan. It really comes down to our approach to safety, and it is pretty simple: teach kids to feel good about themselves, teach parents to reinforce this at home and teach them both safety techniques.

The Hidden Powers Of A Child

Does it really work? Do kids really respond to someone telling them "You Can!" and, "You're Great!" and "Feel Good!"? Do kids begin to believe in themselves when they constantly repeat "I Will Always Do My Best!?"

We think so. Not only do we think so, we believe in it one hundred percent. We hear stories from parents that tell us it does really work, too. A memorable example is from a Mother that told us how her son was constantly the bench warmer on his baseball team. He was always the last one put into the game and the one ignored the most by the coach. The coach would actually tell her, "He just does not have much athletic ability at all."

At one point in the season, about half-way through a session of our Keeping Kids Safe classes, the boy "magically" began hitting the ball well, including a series of homeruns. His batting became the best on the team and his base running and fielding improved, too.

When the Mother was asked by the coach how this "miracle" could have happened the boy interrupted and chimed in, "Because Preston told me I could do anything!"

Is this a miracle? It depends on how you view things. It could be for you. We believe this boy began to realize his Hidden Powers Of A Child. We think the boy simply tapped into what every child has by nature. That is the power within themselves to do and be the best they can be. It just happens to be hidden in a great deal of kids.

Our society takes great care in taking young, wide-eyed, excited children and hammering them into compliant adults. There are societal benefits in doing this. We behave and strive to get along with everyone. We have laws and rules to follow that keep the peace.

At the same, time most children slowly lose their dreams and self-confidence as they grow into adulthood. Doing so begins to bury those powers until they are hidden. How many kids want to grow up to be mid-level managers? Who grows up wanting to struggle with money and finances and making ends meet? Nobody wants these things but they manifest themselves by slowly loosing the understanding that we all have an inner strength and power.

Being the best you can be really isn't a hidden power. It is a power and strength we believe everyone has, even the youngest children. We simply remind kids it is there. We simply bring out the power that kids usually hide under the surface. If they never understood they have it, we show them they do. If they understand they have this great power in themselves, we show them how to build on it even more.

Chapter Summary

- Your child's safety from sexual predators depends on you!

- You must own the responsibility for keeping your child safe.

- You must make sure they learn how to keep themselves safe from sexual predators when you are not around.

- Mentor your child. It gets into making a positive difference by influencing your child to be the best they can be as a person.

- "Commitment" is a very powerful word that can work miracles.
- You must commit to your child's safety.

- View your commitment as the foundation of a lifetime of safety for your child.

- Clarity of focus and vision in teaching your child safety is powerful.

- Clarity of your goal for safety will come with making a commitment to your child's safety program.

- Keep your approach simple, the simpler the better. Clarity comes with simplicity.

- Learn the 5 Secrets To Keeping your child safe.

  - Secret #1: Confidence
  - Secret #2: Empowerment
  - Secret #3: Catch Them Being Good
  - Secret #4: Listening
  - Secret #5: Repetition

- Teach your child the Keeping kids Safe "2 Cardinal Rules."
  - I Will Always Do My Best!
  - I Will Always Say I Can!

- Teach your child to feel good and be able to do it even when they do not feel good.

- Remind your child often, "You Can!"

2

PARENTING SECRETS FOR SAFE KIDS

Parenting Skills For The 21st Century

In teaching your child any of our safety techniques there is one essential thought to keep in the back of your mind at all times: keep it simple. If there is one parenting skill in today's busy, photon light speed world you must have, it is simplicity.

Everything we do at Keeping Kids Safe is so simple with much common sense, it is really hard to make it difficult or challenging to do. At the same time, everything we do is well thought out and based on years of experience. Yet, it is all still effective. It is our "Simplicity By Design" model we used to create our safety program.

You will get better results, great results actually, when you keep your approach to your child's safety as simple as we do. Your parenting skills, while complex in nature, should be able to present the material in a simple, easy way so your kids can understand.

The best parenting skill in today's world for a modern parent is simplicity. It is a 21st century skill.

A simple but effective way to begin teaching your child safety starts with a positive, fun and exciting approach to the subject. Even a serious subject like safety and protection from sexual predators, can be taught to kids in a fun, exciting way with lots of positive reinforcement. We get great results with this approach in our classroom.

Keep your learning sessions with your child fun. Keep them exciting. Keep what you work on with your child in short segments packed full of good feelings and laughter. Positive emotions are very powerful when linked to teaching and learning. When you develop parenting skills that can do this, your child's learning will be accelerated.

Your skills should guide your child through a path of learning our safety techniques rather than boring them with repetitive practice sessions and memorization. Good parenting skills for real child safety relate to guiding, mentoring, and teaching your child.

What we teach in the classroom is very powerful. However, it is still in a classroom. We are effective, but we still are an isolated occurrence once a week in the busy life of a child. Our techniques must be reinforced at home by parents for true, lifelong learning.

Good parenting skills play naturally into reinforcing behaviors you want in your child, easily and effortlessly. Rote repetition should not have to happen, at least with our techniques. Hone your skills and make your child's path to safety easy, fun and effective.

The Key To Parenting Success

"I will always do my best," becomes a lightning rod for growth only if it is incorporated into everyday life. This happens when it is part of family life. It happens when parents and entire families use and embrace the principles of safe kids we have in this book.

Growth and learning also happen at great rates in your child when you let your child express what they naturally possess. This is the key to your success with your parenting skills. Understand your child's innate personality. The more you understand the core nature of your child, their basic personality, the more you can adjust your skills to play into their natural nature. You allow them to learn in an easier manner for them. You also reduce conflict that arises through misunderstanding your child. Just knowing the basics of your child's personality can help you teach them safety in a more effective manner.

You can begin to do this with a simple understanding of the psychological make up of your child.

First, kids are generally:

- Introverted

- Extroverted

Most kids are a mix of these two traits and somewhere in between being introverted or extroverted.

Understanding which of these personalities your child is naturally allows you to guide them through life better. For example, if you deal with your introverted daughter like she was an extrovert you will make your interactions with her more difficult than they need to be. You'll be using skills that she either cannot respond to or responds to badly, perhaps increasing your frustration level. It can quickly spiral out of control.

An introvert is basically a shy person. It is usually a person characterized by concern primarily with his or her own thoughts and feelings.
An extrovert is an outgoing, gregarious person. It is usually a person characterized by extroversion; a person concerned primarily with the physical and social environment.

It is crucial for you to understand that neither one of these personality traits is good or bad. They also do not mean that a child who is an introvert cannot learn to develop skills in the extrovert arena or the other way around.

Most studies show introverts are a minority at around 30% of the population. If your child tends to be introverted, they like quiet activities, especially ones they can do quietly alone. Introverted kids are not antisocial as much as they are exhausted by activities that most kids do like pep clubs, sports teams and church activities.

Highlight and value the introverted qualities of concentration, focus, self discipline, depth, integrity and self knowledge.
Getting your introverted child's attention is pretty easy. Getting them to focus and increase their mental focus abilities is

relatively easy. Teach them with an accent on their ability to work quietly and intensely alone, help them allocate reading time and time to reflect on what you show them. At the same time, making them go out and play with all the other kids can be counter to their natural tendencies.

If your child tends to be extroverted, they are just the opposite of introversion. They are the majority of kids that run around, play games, sports and seem to run on boundless noise. Our society values extroverted children highly. These are the kids that need high energy, excitement and fun built into their learning process consistently. Play into their energy and excitement.

When you grasp the personality type of your child you begin to increase you ability to guide them through life better. You can tool and tune your parenting skills and focus based upon them being extroverted or introverted. You can get results with your child in a manner that is easier for yourself as well as being more effective and easier for your child.

For example, you can guide them in positive directions more easily. When you start to get results, you can increase your effectiveness and adjust your approach as required. More importantly, when you do not get results you can adjust your approach until you get results.

The Amazing Skill That Works Miracles

Our kids talk to us all the time. We listen, and we talk back to them. It happens everyday, but how much of these conversations and interactions do you really understand? Are you really hearing what your child is saying from their perspective or are you interpreting their words into your adult way of thinking and perceiving?

Learn to understand and interpret what your child is saying, in their words, in their meanings. This is an invaluable parenting skill called "Listening" and is at the center of any safety program for your child. You need to be able to decipher exactly what they are saying and meaning when they come to you with an issue.

Good listening skills are part of an array of good parenting skills. They benefit you in many ways as a parent that go beyond safety such as making life easier with less conflict for all involved in your family. It's what we call a secondary benefit of following our safety program. Good listening skills ease miscommunication and can eliminate a lot of misunderstandings that sap energy.

There are two keys in listening to your child effectively. One, learn to understand their words. How your child uses words and what your child means with them is very different from how you use those same words.

Start to create in your mind a dictionary of definitions of words your child uses. Understand and know their definition of terms and how they apply them at their age. Keep a watch as to how these definitions and uses change as they grow.

Two, take the time to stop, sit down and look your child directly in the eyes when they have something important to tell you. This simple gesture subtly embeds in your child the fact that you are there for them to go to any time they need to do so. In terms of safety, they need to know they can confidently go to you with anything. They need to have a safe, secure feeling that you will listen to them.

Yes, every parent today is just too busy but we are talking about 5 minutes of your time! What is your child's safety worth to you? Yes, your child comes and interrupts you numerous times a day. You have the intuition however, to know when it is really important. You know when you have to stop what you are doing, sit down and listen to them. Take the time to do it.

Finally, whatever your child tells you, stay calm, listen intently and do not interrupt them. Especially if your child says something that is disconcerting, you must learn to listen to them calmly.

The bottom line in safety is, you are teaching your child to come to you if ever they are approached or touched by a sexual predator.

You are showing your child that you, as their parent, are the trusted confidant they can go to, when anything uncomfortable happens to them, like being approached by a sexual predator. It is critical in their ability to keep themselves safe that you become their "go to person."

Secrets To Deciphering The Silence

Your child also communicates in nonverbal ways, too. We all do. It's a great asset to have in being able to read your child's body language. It enhances your parenting skills and ability to teach them our safety techniques.

This ability, coupled with understanding their personality traits and good listening skills gives you a very powerful set of parenting skills. Again, the more skills you have the better you can teach, mentor and guide them in life and personal safety when you are not around.

Nonverbal communication is very complicated. However, there are some simple patterns and gestures you can understand in your child that helps you communicate better with them, especially when they are not so talkative. Observe their posture. It will tell you more than their words, sometimes.

It is not so hard to read the basics of body language. Keep in mind, these are generalities, but they will give you a basic understanding of what your child is really saying:

- Crossing arms and legs while standing is a defensive gesture.

- If they want to tell you they really don't like a person or what you may be saying, they narrow their eyes, tilt their head back and to the side and keep their lips together. Folding arms always helps in communicating dislike

- The main difference between sitting and standing is that

sitting is a relatively
defenseless position,
therefore almost forcing trust
and empathy.

- Fibbing usually entails a lack
  of eye contact and excessive
  hand movements.

- Shifting from foot to foot
  shows worrying about getting
  found out. Also, it indicates
  that they want to go
  somewhere else to get away
  so that no guilty expressions
  are spotted like looking out
  the door, backing up towards
  the door, half-facing the
  person and half-facing the
  door, etc.

- Rubbing the back of the head
  can demonstrate comforting
  oneself when saddened. It
  also shows impatience.

- Standing with arms crossed
  shows a sense of being
  'closed'. It can also show
  anger, stubbornness and
  assertiveness.

- Standing with one hand on
  hip is the opposite to the
  above. It's suggestive of
  'openness'.

- Inspecting fingernails indicates boredom or vanity.

- Hands clasped together or hands placed one over the other indicates deference and humility.

What does this mean for you? Simply, it offers another communication tool for you to utilize in parenting your child to true safety for a lifetime. Is your child bored when you are teaching them something? Spice up the excitement or do it another time. Is your child angry with you? Chances are they are not going to pay much attention to any safety lessons for a while. Catching your child fibbing is a good time to reinforce honesty and rewards for being forthright.

Knowing these characteristics simply adds another element to your growing arsenal of parenting skills for better child safety.

Catch Them Being Good

It is so easy for parents to catch their kids doing the things they shouldn't be doing. It's almost natural, too easy, for parents to highlight these negative things they see.

Make an effort to highlight the good things your child does.

We teach safety to kids from a position of positive reinforcement and personal growth. We think we get better results with this approach. We "Catch Kids Being Good" and make it a point to praise them.

Kids love praise. They especially love it when it comes from you, Mom and Dad. Your child lives for your approval. Approve of them. Be lavish with your praise. Do it consistently. Do it regularly. Do it with feeling.

The Nucleus Of Safety

What does it mean when all of these skills come together? It means a safer child. These skills improve your child's learning of our safety techniques. They can be safe for a lifetime if you use them when you teach them the actual techniques we will show you.

Good parenting skills can make your child safer and they also have benefits for your family, too. Good safety and good families are all intimately interrelated. They go hand-in-hand.

We call the blending of safe kids and good

families, the "Nucleus Of Safety."
Maximizing its effectiveness depends on good parenting skills and commitment to being the best you can be, for both parents and kids.

Our Nucleus Of Safety is for all families. We know that 65% of families in America today are headed by single parents. We know there are multi-racial adoptive families, foster families and grandparents and aunts and uncles raising kids. The Nucleus Of Safety is for all of you. It is for anyone raising kids or anyone who cares about kids. It is for all of you.

This may seem eons away from stopping sexual predators. It is not. Our approach to safety starts with us focusing on helping make better kids. When we do that, we can help make them safer kids. While we focus on stopping sexual predators, we also can capitalize on what we teach and improve other areas in your child's life.

So then, what really is this "Nucleus Of Safety?" It is families coming together to stay one step in front of sexual predators and stop them cold. It is our efforts and yours together that will make this world a little safer for every child. Five minutes a day means better kids, safer kids, better families.

Chapter Summary

- If there is one parenting skill to have today, it is simplicity.

- A simple but effective way to begin teaching your child safety starts with a positive, fun and exciting approach to the subject.

- Keep your learning sessions with your child fun. Keep them exciting. Keep what you work on with your child in short segments packed full of good feelings and laughter.

- Understand which basic personality type your child is:
  - Introverted

  - Extroverted

- Most kids are a mix of these two traits and somewhere in between being introverted or extroverted.

- Understanding which of these personalities your child is naturally allows you to guide them through life better.

- Learn to understand and interpret what your

child is saying, in their words, in their meanings.

- "Listening" is at the center of any safety program for your child.

- Learn to understand how your child uses words.

- Take the time to stop, sit down and look your child directly in the eyes when they have something important to tell you.

- Learn to listen to your child calmly and quietly without interrupting them.

- Learn to read your child's basic body language to understand what they are really saying.

- Catch your child being good and make it a point to praise them often.

3

THE GROWING CANCER OF SEXUAL PREDATORS

Predators That Prowl Our Neighborhoods

Predators are difficult for most of us to recognize. Any parent will gladly stand guard in their yard or take their turn patrolling the street in front of the house watching out for predators. However, watching out for sexual predators searching for your child is just not that simple.

First of all, the media does all of us a disservice. Yes, it is trendy to blame the media for all kinds of ills. When it comes to predators, we are not blaming the media for a problem, as much as alerting you to the shortcomings of movies, television shows and yes, even newscasts.

Movies and television shoes depict predators as if they came from Mars. We see dirty, leering, filthy adults that would make sewer rats cringe, as they slink and lurk behind garbage cans.

Newscasts have become focused more on ratings and selling advertising than hard real news. There are just too many confusing pieces of information and messages out there for most parents to filter through. Unfortunately, a lot of the information on child safety, although well intended, is old, outdated, useless or just plain wrong. Many ideas and notions about sexual predators are just plain wrong, too.

Who are these predators and how can you recognize them? You really can't. If there is one message for you to understand, it is this one. Sexual predators look like everyone. They look like your neighbors. They look like the people at the grocery store. They look like everyday, normal individuals.

What to do about stopping sexual predators comes from knowledge and education. It's all about having a trusted source that can filter through the maze of information and disinformation for you. We're that filter for you.

First, sexual predators are difficult to spot. Not only do they look like us but they drive vehicles just like we do, too. They drive family vehicles that are like every other car on the road.

What we are saying is this: there is no real way to go about your daily life and be able to spot sexual predators. This is why we teach kids the added advantage of keeping themselves safe. This is why we arm kids with all kinds of tool and techniques so they can deal with people, people in general, so that if in the end they shed their disguise as normal people and reveal the hidden sexual predator, your child can be safe.

The Jeffrey Dahmer's, John Wayne Gasey's and Ted Bundy's of this world were described as "the nice guys next door." All of them were prowling predators no one spotted.

Discovering How Predators Prowl For Kids

We know that sexual predators search for the child that they see as weak, sad and unhappy. It's the kid with the shuffling feet, head drooping and eyes fixed to the ground. It's the child that appears they are in need of a friend. The predator wants an easy target when the time is "right."

For the most part, predators are not interested in any kind of visible, noisy or public struggle that brings attention to their nefarious deeds.

In fact, many predators choose to befriend a child first. They choose to develop a dependent relationship with a child that appears to be in need of a close friend. It could be a sad, unhappy child. The predator then offers them gifts, ideas, or simple emotional comfort that makes the child feel better. The process slowly introduces sexual context and content into their interactions and conversations.

Some predators immediately engage in sexually explicit conversation with children right from the start. Online or Internet sexual predators may collect and trade child-pornographic images. Others online may seek real face to face meetings with the kids they emailed or connected with in chat rooms or social blogs.

There is no one profile. Predators cunningly exploit weakness and naiveté. They will work very hard at driving a wedge between a child and their family. Predators will even accentuate any minor problems at home that your child might have, again befriending them and driving that wedge into the family structure.

A confident child represents more of a challenge, a problem, someone who will be hard to manipulate, for the sexual predator. Confident kids will also be uncooperative. They understand better, even if they cannot articulate their feelings, that something or someone is "just not right" and will avoid them or stay away.

Today's Dangerous World

Today's world is a dangerous place. Today's dangerous world is very different than anything seen before. It's dangerous for adults. It is very dangerous for our precious children. This sad truth is a reality however, one that you must accept and deal with in order to keep your child safe from sexual predators.

Many parents today just don't know how to keep their kids safe in a modern world. There is nothing wrong with that. They grew up themselves with their parents warning of "Don't talk to strangers!" when they were a child heading out the door to play. It was truly useless information to the child back then as it is today, but somehow made the parents feel their children were safe.

Many parents, although they are adults now, still think like this. Today, however, this kind of thinking can not only keep your child unsafe, it may put them at risk as a target for sexual predators. This kind of thinking can really endanger your child.

"This guy has to be a bad stranger," or "Stay away from weirdoes!" seems like it has to help. The sad news, however, is it is useless. The fact is, many parents today have no idea how to keep themselves safe let alone teach their children safety from sexual predators.

Telling your child not to talk to strangers or telling your child any neighbor can be trusted is a recipe for danger. If you go around like this you are playing with odds that you child will not be the one ever approached by a sexual predator. That is roulette with your child's life. So, we'll help you change your ideas about child safety. We'll help you teach your child to be safer in today's world with a little education and knowledge.

The Enormity Of The Problem

Let's start with understanding the problem of sexual predators today. Let's understand just how big the problem really is. The FBI states on their February 2007 website statistics:

- 1 of 5 girls will be sexually molested before her 18th birthday.

- 1 of 6 boys will be sexually molested before his 18th birthday.

- 1 of 5 children has been propositioned for sex over the Internet.

- 2 of 3 sexual abuses are perpetrated against teenagers or younger children.

- 90% of sexual assaults are committed against someone the perpetrator knows.

- The median age for male molestation victims under 18 is 9.8 years old.

- The median age for female molestation victims under 18 is 9.6 years old.

- There are 400,000 new victims of sexual assault every year.

- There are over 550,000 registered sex offenders in the US.

- There are over 100,000 sex offenders that fail to register in the US.

- 76% of serial rapists claim they were molested as children.

- Over 40% of male juvenile delinquents were molested as children.

These statistics are unacceptable. Some studies show in the last three years an increase in sexual abuse statistics, as well. Lowering these statistics, helping solve this growing cancer, starts with you, Keeping Kids Safe and your child. Teach your kids our simple techniques in this book.

The problem with statistics is that is neutralizes the affects of abuse on the people that are touched by it. Statistics make the victims depersonalized and faceless.

The victims, the children, are the ones that really suffer and abuse will affect them for a lifetime. Abuse affects all that it touches, too, including family and friends. Some victims struggle their entire life to overcome the horror of abuse.

Statistics are fine to make our point. But the real point is the poignant stories of the victims. Even in our field, we are constantly struck by the number of individuals who come up to us and tell us their stories of their lives and the negative effects foisted upon them by sexual predators.

Basic Fears To Face

When we hold seminars, classes, meetings or even go to business gatherings, people line up to tell us their stories of how they or someone they know, were abused.

It takes great courage for them, for anyone, to face the realty of sexual abuse. We applaud their courage and take the time to listen to each one. They are helping stop predators cold along with us and each of their stories is important.

> *I was recently in Orlando, Florida and had a short slide show presentation, and I put up a slide of our long on the screen behind the stage.*
>
> *I showed the slide, introduced myself and said, "I'm here to STOP PREDATORS COLD!*
>
> *The audience instantly stood up and clapped and cheered. It took close to 5 minutes for*

them to quiet down and sit again so I could continue.

I was in a room with complete strangers.

I was blown away.

Afterwards everyone in the room lined up to talk to me. The program I was part of had to shut down for almost an hour so I could meet and chat with everyone. In the line at least every fourth or fifth person told me their own personal story of abuse.

I sat down later that day and had lunch with two women who each related to me their stories of their children who were abused. While each woman had never met each other until this time, their stories were sadly similar. They told me how they pursued the predators into the legal system. They chased them despite their family's insistence on quietly ignoring the problem. They spent years pursuing and chasing the predator without hesitating for a second. I found myself admiring them and thanking them for their spirit, persistence and courage.

For weeks after this meeting I was in touch with many of the individuals as this book unfolded. I became even more driven to get this out so I could help as many kids as possible.

In connecting with one individual, who had marketed his book successfully and in a similar manner, he told me, "I cannot talk to you anymore. This is just too close to me. Please respect my feelings."

I wrote him back and said, "Thank you. I will. I wish you the best."

Why am I telling you all this?

Even with my involvement in Keeping Kids Safe, even knowing what I know today, I am still shocked at the depth and breath of child abuse in our world.

It touches everyone in some way. Sexual predators must be stopped.

- Joyce Jackson

It Could Happen To You

If the is one message we want to get across to all parents, it is, "Be Proactive." Never make the mistake of thinking a sexual predator could never abuse your child.

We are not fomenting paranoia. We are, however, touting the reality of today's world. Teach your child our safety ideas and techniques. They are really fun to learn and do as games, even with a serious topic like safety. Teach your child to keep themselves safe for a lifetime.

The Dangers Of False Ideas

We're going to dispel some of the false ideas about child safety. There are a lot of websites around today, a lot of ideas and a lot of methods being taught for child safety. Some of these ideas are just downright false. Be wary of any of our "Top Three False Ideas About Safety." They may not only not keep your child safe but endanger them by a false sense of security in both you and your child.

False Safety Idea #1: Don't Talk To Strangers.

If we didn't talk to strangers we'd never make new friends. Just answer this, did you talk to the cashier at the gas station today? Did you exchange pleasantries at the grocery store with the check out clerk? We talk to strangers all the time. We need to talk to strangers in everyday life or we would be isolated. Our lives, everyday, are all about interacting with people that we don't know very well. These people are strangers.

It's pretty confusing then, to tell you child not to talk with strangers when they see you doing this all the time.

A stranger is simply someone you don't know very well. Knowing someone well means you visit them in their home, spend time with their family and they with yours.

We talk to strangers all the time and its "OK" for our kids to talk to strangers, too, as long as they do it with some additional safety techniques, like an effective Circle Of Safety.

A stranger is someone you don't know very well. Therefore, teach your child this simple idea of a stranger. Then teach them to deal effectively with all strangers. Then, if a stranger turns out to be a bad stranger, they can keep themselves safe and escape.

False Safety Idea #2: Teach Your Child An 8' to 10' Circle Of Safety
Probably one of the worst things you can do is tell your child to stay 10 feet away from strangers.

Do this exercise:

> Get 10 feet away from you kid and blitz in on them. Surprise them. By the time they realize what is happening and turn to run you can grab them.

This basic Circle Of Safety is true in theory. It is true as long as no one moves. This is the problem with most child safety programs that teach a Circle of Safety. In situations where kids are grabbed by predators no one is standing still.

We take the idea of the Circle of Safety one giant step further, five to ten feet further, to be exact.

We teach a 15' to 20' Circle Of Safety. Why? It's pretty simple: the standard 8' to 10' Circle Of Safety does not work if an adult blitzes in full speed to grab a kid. Kids need time to react and run at kid speed and still stay ahead of a running adult. The 8' to

10' circle does not give them enough reaction time.

<u>False Safety Idea #3:</u> Yelling "Help!" When In Trouble Will Get People's Attention

Yelling "Help!' when in trouble or grabbed by a predator will not get a child help. Most kids yell when they play. A lot of kids yell, "Help!" when they play and repeat it several times at the top of their voice. We have all come to ignore this.

We teach kids to yell, "Fire!" when they are grabbed or in real danger. It is a word that gets people's attention. It is a word that can get them help, fast.

Extreme Predators

There are, much to all of our horror, child predators that will go to any measure, any extreme measure to abduct a child. These heinous individuals will use weapons, sneak attacks, hidden drugs and teams of helpers to grab and abduct a child.

We call these people Extreme Predators.

To thwart these people we have to get very creative and extremely effective in our techniques ourselves. We use Extreme Safety techniques we teach our advanced students in order to arm them with the ability to keep themselves safe under any circumstances.

The first rule in dealing with Extreme Predators is to never leave the place you are at with any stranger. It is the first step in stifling any abduction. A child must understand that whatever transpires, their first rule of safety is to never leave the area they are at with their abductor.

There are a number of things they can do to accomplish this, even if the predator has a weapon.

If a child finds themselves starting to be grabbed and dragged away we teach them to drop to the ground and grab something with both arms and legs. Grab a mail box. Grab a sign post. If there is nothing for them to grab onto we teach them to grab hold of the legs of the actual predator.

We show them how to completely wrap both arms and legs around any object and draw their hands in tight to their chest making their grasp even more effective. All the while we teach them to yell "Fire! Fire!"

If the predator displays a weapon such as a knife or a gun a real challenge exists. We teach kids to fake a seizure, an asthma attack or a choking fit. Basically, they fall to the ground faking a dire medical condition, anything, to throw the predator off their mission of abduction and allow the child a chance to stay in the area.

Why is staying in the area **SO CRITICAL?**

It is about survival for the child at this point. It comes down to simply saving their life. The staggering facts from the FBI show that most abducted children are eventually killed by their abductors. A child who can figure out a way to stay in the area will increase their chances of staying alive.

Yes, these are extreme measures. Life and death situations call for these measures and these may save just one more child's life.

Chapter Summary

- What to do about stopping sexual predators comes from knowledge and education.

- Sexual predators are everywhere in today's world. There is no real way to go about your daily life and be able to spot sexual predators. This is why we teach kids the added advantage of keeping themselves safe.

- Predators prowl for easy victims.

- There is no one predator profile. Predators cunningly exploit weakness and naiveté. They will work very hard at driving a wedge between a child and their family.

- The victims, the children, are the ones that really suffer and abuse will affect them for a lifetime.

- Abuse affects all that it touches, too, including family and friends. Some victims struggle their entire life to overcome the horror of abuse.

- Never make the mistake of thinking a sexual predator could never abuse your child.

- False ideas about safety may not only not keep your child safe but endanger them by a false sense of security in both you and your child.

  - <u>False Safety Idea #1:</u> Don't Talk To Strangers

  - <u>False Safety Idea #2:</u> Teach Your Child An 8' to 10' Circle Of Safety

  - <u>False Safety Idea #3:</u> Yelling "Help!" When In Trouble Will Get People's Attention

- We use Extreme Safety techniques to arm kids with the ability to keep themselves safe under any circumstances, including Extreme Predators.

- The first rule in dealing with Extreme Predators is to never leave the place you are at with any stranger.

- Teach your child how to completely wrap both arms and legs around any object and draw their hands in tight to their chest making their grasp even more effective.

- If the predator displays a weapon such as a knife or a gun teach your child to fake a seizure, an asthma attack or a choking fit and fall to the ground.

4

HIDDEN POWERS OF A CHILD

The Immutable Laws Of Safety

There are certain things we have learned that we just have to do in order to teach kids to keep themselves safe. For example, we have to talk with and play with the kids. "With" the kids and not "To" the kids is a crucial element in teaching them effectively.

We can talk all day long to kids but it is truly about getting through to each child, in order to get them to learn safety techniques. It is truly about kids understanding what it is we are saying so they can learn how to keep themselves safe.

We have discovered certain Immutable Laws Of Safety we must follow in order to insure that kids, who need to learn to keep themselves safe, understand and learn what we are teaching them.

Law #1: Get Their Attention

No matter what you want to teach to kids, there is one thing you have to do: get their attention.

With personal safety issues, this is critical. And, there's not a lot of room for error with this topic. Kid's lives are at stake. We take this Law very seriously. We get the kid's attention from the second they walk into our classroom.

Not only do we have to get their attention, we have to hold it for 45 minutes. We do this by intentionally creating a fun and exciting environment for the kids. The children have to be happy, excited and want to be in class. Sometimes they are naturally excited and full of anticipation. Sometimes they are "flat" and tired.

It's our job, regardless of their energy level, to get their attention and make the class fun and exciting. When we do that, even a topic as serious as personal safety, can be taught in a fun and exciting way.

This Law is the first key in teaching children anything. We always make it a point to pump up the excitement and fun so the first order of business is getting kids attention.

Law #2: Build Their Confidence
We've already touched upon confidence as a key to safer kids. We cannot emphasize it enough. Once we have the kid's attention, we immediately start right in with teaching them to appear and learn to be more confident.

Your child is less of a target for predators by walking around looking more confident and happy, even when they don't necessarily feel that way. Confident kids are not an easy target and that is why they are safer. With their shoulders back, head high and eyes alert to the environment around them, they appear to be more of a problem for a predator when you are not around.

If you child is walking home from school with their head held high and tuned into their environment with sharp mental focus, they should be able to see a potentially dangerous situation and avoid it.

If your child cannot consciously understand what is wrong but feels uneasy around a certain adult, they can leave the area and tell you about it. They are listening to their gut reaction and following their natural instincts to safety. Confidence in oneself is one of the crucial keys to a safe child.

How do you build confidence in your child? One of the things that works very well is positive motivation. Using positive motivation rather than negative criticism to motivate your child is a great way to build confidence.

In its simplest form, positive motivation is going out of your way to praise your child for the good things you see them doing. Praise them for the many small good things they do as well as the larger ones. Praise them profusely and more importantly, mean it when you say it. Do it without qualifications.

Your true parenting skill comes in praising them for their effort, not your expectations. Stay away from the, "This is 'OK' but..." mentality. Start by being aware that most children aren't going to perform any task to adult expectations. If your child does not perform up to your standards, it is vitally important you still complement them on the effort they did do. If nothing else, thank them for their effort or for at least listening to you and trying to execute the task. "Thank you for listening to me," is very powerful.

Your child lives to please you which is why positive motivation works so well with children. At the same time, when you ask your child to do something and follow with telling them they have failed at it in some way to pull it off, it is berating them for their performance. It can be devastating to a child's self image.

In reality, if you ask them to do something and they do it to their ability, your child should be praised and complimented for their execution of the task. In reality, they did what you asked them to do. You as the parent should then guide them into better execution of the task next time.

Building confidence happens over time with consistent effort on your part. It grows as your child does. It is never too early to begin building confidence and never too late to start.

Law #3: A Stranger Is Someone You Don't Know Very Well

It is very important to know who is a stranger. We talk about this time and time again in many ways and re-emphasize it here. At Keeping Kids Safe, a "stranger" is simply someone you don't know very well.

We teach kids to deal effectively with strangers, all strangers. For true safety from sexual predators, it does not matter if a stranger is good or bad, just that they are strangers. So, it comes down to what really is a definition of a stranger and how to deal with all strangers in general.

For a child, the simpler the concept, the easier it is to understand and do what needs to be done. That is the idea behind learning to deal with strangers, all types of strangers. Our idea of a stranger being someone you don't know very well is simple enough for even a child of four to understand.

And there are a lot of strangers out there. The world is full of strangers. We run into more strangers everyday than we do close friends. If you or your kids never talked to strangers they would literally never talk to very many people.

A STRANGER IS SOMEONE YOU DON'T KNOW VERY WELL.

It is that simple.

We live in a society in a social world as human beings that are very sociable. We need to talk to strangers in order to make new friends, new business contacts or future relationships. The point is, we talk to strangers all the time!

Here is how pervasive strangers really are: do you chat with the check out clerk at the grocery store? Do you exchange pleasantries with the pharmacist? Do you wave and say "Hi!" to the neighbor on the next block in the health club?

Of course you do. We all do.

However, have you been in their homes? Have you had dinner with them and met their families? Do you spend time with them on a one-to-one basis each week?

Most likely, you have not. Therefore, they are strangers.
A stranger is someone you don't know very well. And the definition of "well" is knowing and spending time with them and their family. You spend the time with them within the confines of your or their home on a regular basis.

Now, who really is a stranger?

We are surrounded by strangers every day. When you understand this definition of a stranger you can begin to realize not only how but how easy it is for a child to begin to understand this.

Law #4: It's "OK" To Talk To Strangers
A stranger is someone you don't know very well and it's "OK" to talk to them. Again, something we mentioned before but is so critical is worth mentioning again.

Our techniques, tips and strategies are unique, effective and yes, controversial because they are based upon this idea that a stranger is someone you don't know very well and that you can talk to them.

Again, this is so simple, we find that children can grasp these two simple ideas and understand them. They know what these two things mean in their brain and at their age.

Do this: do a search on Google for "kid safety program." There are millions of links and websites out there that want to teach you about bad strangers and don't talk to strangers and how strangers will hurt you.

Confused? Just think about what this does to the thinking process in a child. Most kids right now, today, including your child do not know who the real threats are. Your child and many kids out there are confused about predators and real threats.

We clarify this down to the simple truth of who is a stranger for a child at their level of thinking: it is someone you don't know very well.

And here's another shock for you: your child's teacher at school is a stranger, too.

Most of us do not sit down in the homes of our kids' school teachers. We interact with them more than most people but we still do not know them very well as a person.

The school situation is "OK" however because of the number of other kids and adults around and the environment. But it is important to understand the idea of a stranger.

We talk to strangers all the time. We need to talk to strangers in everyday life or we would be isolated.

It is all about people that we don't know very well and knowing someone well means we visit them in their homes, we spend time with them in their homes and we know their families and they know ours.

It simply comes down to how we teach kids to deal with strangers. The simplest way your child can understand what a stranger is, is by applying this easy rule: "If your child would not get into a car with the person and let them drive them somewhere, they are a stranger."

Law #5: When A Stranger Approaches Engage A Circle Of Safety

If your child finds themselves alone somewhere and a stranger approaches, teach them to engage in a Circle Of Safety. Again, to emphasize, teach them to do this with any stranger when they are alone. Additionally, teach them an "effective" Circle Of Safety.

An effective Circle Of Safety for an elementary school child is 15' to 20' in diameter. Most safety programs teach an 8' to 12' Circle Of Safety. We expand it. The simple fact is, most young children cannot turn and run away fast enough in the event a large adult runs in full stride at them with a 8' to 12' Circle Of Safety. With the expanded version we teach even the youngest child can do two things very well: one, talk and communicate effectively with the stranger from 15' to 20' without shouting. Two, they have plenty of distance to turn and run to safety even if a large, fast adult charges at them.

If a stranger approaches or gets too close to a child's Circle of Safety, kids yell a single command while raising their arm up into a stop-like gesture. The command is, "STOP! I'm not supposed to get close to Strangers!"

If the stranger continues toward the child we then again teach kids to turn and run away to someone for help. If the stranger simply has a question like, "I'm looking for the hospital" they can still ask the child from a distance. The 15' to 20' Circle Of Safety allows for normal conversation.

They can also recognize what the child is doing and move away, again as most responsible people will do when this happens. We teach kids to never let any stranger in their Circle of Safety. If it happens then we teach them to turn and run. Be aware that these are definitions based on when your child finds them self alone with an approaching stranger. Again, with the example at school, your child will not engage their teacher with a Circle Of Safety, even if they are a stranger by our definition. Why is this "OK?" Because the school environment has many other people, both children and adults, present that provides safety around strangers. It's the same with summer camps, after school groups and sports activities. You can easily make this distinction for your child and they will understand.

Law #6: Speak In A Power Voice

We teach kids in danger to speak with their "Power Voice." Everyone has one of these and the technique is in teaching a child to use a strong voice that comes from the abdomen, not the throat. Each child is capable of this type of voice, even children as young as four years old.

When kids yell, and most adults too, they yell from their throat. We teach kids to yell from their belly. This belly yell is easy to do. Put your hand on your abdomen and push out with your stomach muscles. Do it again and huff out a breath with it. Do it one more time and this time push out your breath and make a sound with it.

It sounds like a deep "Huh!"

More importantly, it comes out with a measure of strength and power. This is the kid's safety Power Voice. We practice this a lot with kids and tell them to, "Bounce Your Voice off The Walls!" Again, it comes from the abdomen, not the throat and when done correctly the difference is astonishing.

Kids will need to learn this voice in case they ever need to use it in a threatening situation. It will get people's attention when it is used.

Once again, how do you teach your child this at home? First and foremost, make it a game. Start with making it fun,
Hey Susie, want to play a game?" works better than, "Susie, let's practice our Power Voice."

Get your child's "Buy in" to the game to get their attention.

Then add an element of success in it. A win-lose element in it works magic for your child such as, "If I win I get a cupcake and if you win you get the cupcake" will heighten their interest. We call playing the Power Voice game, "bouncing the voice off the wall with fun."

As you do this make sure you keep eye contact with your child, keep the game short and keep it fun. Get creative with your games and come up with something fun your child can enjoy!

Law #7: Yell "FIRE!" When In A Dangerous Situation

Yelling "Fire!" when in a dangerous or threatening situation will get a child help fast.

When a child turns and runs from their Circle Of Safety they need to get the attention of someone that will help them immediately. We teach kids to yell, "Fire!" for many reasons. One, kids are always yelling when they play. One of their favorite things to yell when playing is "Help!" They also tend to yell "Help!" in very high pitched, throaty voices. Adults and other family members quickly learn to ignore these yells of "Help!"

If a child yells "Help!" and really means it, chances are they will be ignored. They will not get the help they need when they really need it.

Why?

Cries of "Help!" do not get people's attention because "Help!" simply does not say anything. It is ambiguous. It provides no information. "Help!" tells us someone is in trouble but it gives no details. Most people will hesitate to get involved because we fear for our own safety with cries of "Help!"

We teach kids to yell, "Fire!" when they are in need of real help. The word "Fire!" gets anyone's attention immediately. It is a word that is rarely, if ever, ignored. It, as a word by itself, gives details. Even if it is yelled in a high pitched throaty voice it will get people's attention.

Law #8: Listen To Your Belly Brain
We teach kids that they have two brains, the one in their head and one in their belly.

We call the one in the belly the "Belly Brain."

We teach kids to listen to their "Belly Brain." For adults, this is that visceral, gut feeling that is always right. Kids have this gut feeling too, but they need some help in learning how to listen to it and use it to keep themselves safe.

We take time to show them how the Belly Brain works for them and how to listen to it. We help kids distinguish between and understand the difference in their "Head Brain" and their "Belly Brain." We also show them that their Belly Brain is always right.

In the class, we show the kids how their "Head Brain" can sometimes trick them. We reinforce the Belly Brain as the alarm clock for potentially dangerous situations. Kids can learn to recognize the uneasiness in their stomach without panic, alarm and worry. So, we teach them to see potential danger calmly and avoid it with any number of safety techniques we teach.

When kids tune into their "Belly Brain" they are more tuned in to detecting uncomfortable situations, situations with questionable adults and inappropriate behavior.

Kids naturally feel uncomfortable with inappropriate questions and behaviors they are around. We simply show them how to be alert to it with their "Belly Brain" and immediately take action when they feel it talk to them.

When kids learn to listen to their "Belly Brain" we show them how to follow up by immediately acting on it. That action is as simple and effective as leaving the area where they "feel funny" and telling a trusted adult like Mom and Dad about how they feel and who they were with when they feel their "Belly Brain" talk to them.

Law# 9: When Grabbed By A Predator, Yell, Point and Look

In the horrible event a child is grabbed by a sexual predator we teach them to stay calm, focus, do three things.

The first is to yell with a Power Voice:

- **FIRE! FIRE! He's Not My Dad!**

The yell changes based upon who is grabbing. For an adult woman:

- **FIRE! FIRE! She's Not My Mom!**

For a teenage boy:
- **FIRE! FIRE! He's Not My Brother!**

For a teenage girl:

- **FIRE! FIRE! She's Not My Sister!**

Two, we teach children to look directly into the predator's eyes and point at them with their free hand while yelling. The reason for this scenario and specific technique is simple: this type of yell, look and pointing is different from when Mom or Dad take a child home.

Almost every kid at the park on weekends screams and yells when the parents tell them its time to go home. They whine, they cry, they dig in their heels and when Mom or Dad grabs their wrist they pull back yelling, "No! No! No!" There are no kids being pulled home by parents that are yelling, "FIRE! FIRE! He's Not My Dad!"

Three, we teach the child to perform this yell sequence until they get help. It's more than a one time thing. It's a continual sequence of abdominal yells, techniques and movements.

Four, we teach kids to look directly into the predators eyes while executing these safety techniques. It gives the child an extra edge in that most kids do not look adults directly into their eyes and it increase their chance of being noticed. It also may throw the predator off for a split second with a child penetrating them with a strong gaze. A split second like this could afford a child an escape to safety.

The Ultimate Safety Secret

The one thing, above all else, that is paramount in your child being able to keep themselves safe, is mental focus. It is so important, that we call it the Power Of Focus.

Our program starts with the Power Of Focus because it is paramount in having children develop the ability to protect themselves. Your child must have the mental ability to focus in order to get out of threatening situations.

The fact is, if your child cannot mentally focus they will not be able to keep themselves safe. Whenever a threatening situation is developing your child needs to be able to spot it before they are caught in it. Focus. If your child is caught in a dangerous situation they need to get out of it. Focus. If your child is grabbed they need to escape. They need to focus. Mental Focus.

We teach children, as young as four, the Power Of Focus. With teaching them focus abilities, comes an increased ability to concentrate, even for even the youngest children. With increased focus comes the ability to stay calm in a crisis, assess a viable escape and execute it to complete safety. Our methods can improve your child's focus. We can get effective results with very young and small children.

The type of focus we are talking about is a little different than what you may be thinking. As your child grows, they encounter situations, such as sports, that teach them focus. Children can get very good focusing on a specific thing, like a technique in sports. Personal safety is different.

Personal safety requires mental focus before any safety techniques can be learned. In sports, focus is a byproduct of the activity. In safety, each unfolding danger situation is fluid. There may never be anything repeatable like in a sports activity. We teach mental focus as an independent activity so kids can learn to be calm, look at a fluid and dynamic situation and be able to get themselves out of it.

This works and does elicit results, again, even in the youngest children. We teach children to develop and extend their focus abilities. With age appropriate exercises and encouragement kids can learn to do this very well. We do this best with games. Mental focus is a child's ability to understand something. Understanding enables them to react appropriately to it, like reacting appropriately to threatening situations. You can increase this focus ability at home by playing mental focus games.

One such game we use is our "Powers of Understanding" Game. Here, we ask a child to look down at their shoes, then give them a list of four or five things to do. We ask the child to repeat the list back. More often than not, they cannot repeat the entire list. Then we ask the child to look us directly in the eyes and give them a new list. When we ask them to repeat it back to us, most kids get it correct. They also can repeat it in the order given them. Getting this focus game down for a child depends on their ability to look you in the eyes, so make sure you tune into this.

Be creative with this game, too. Sometimes we call this the "Shopping Game" and ask the kids what they want to shop for to help in getting their "buy-in." If they say "Toys!" we say, "OK! You're going to the toy store and you're going to get a doll, a green bike a big blue ball and a dump truck. Now, what are you going to get at the toy store?"

You can also use a chalk board and write down the items if you wish, and then ask them to say the list back to you. Just make it fun.

We're only talking 5 or 10 minutes games. Longer and the child will not want to play in the future. You can create any game, just use the same scenario mentioned before: get their attention, get their buy in, make it simple, short, fun and exciting with a winning prize at the end.

Improve This And Your Child Will Be Safer

Teach your child these safety techniques in this book, but teach them in their own words. You have to teach your child by talking to your child in words they understand. Communicate safety to them in their words and you'll teach them faster and better.

Adults talk to children all day long. We have all seen the cartoons that show adults as nothing more than noisy "Blah! Blah!

Blah!" nonsense sounds around children. They are not far from the truth to kids.

We've learned that talking with kids rather than talking to them works. We relate to kids in a manner that is fun, even on a serious topic such as safety. It makes the learning process faster, easier and more effective, for the children.
We talk to them in terms and words they use and they understand. We sit on the floor with the kids so we can be one of them among the group. We look them in the eyes at their eye level instead of standing up looking down at them.

We teach them how to stay safe from strangers. We teach them what a stranger really is and how to stay out of danger with any stranger. We also show them how to communicate with a stranger in order to keep safe. A lot of people do what we do but we do it more effectively in a manner that gets through to the kids. It's all about teaching kids to keep themselves safe.

Defining Ultimate Safety

So, we talk to and teach the kids in manner that gets right to them. At the same time we need the parents on board with everything we do, too. Ultimate safety comes from parents.

Parents are integral in our Keeping Kids Safe program. Kids get the most out of what we teach them when we engage the parents as part of the teaching and learning process.

First, kids want to please their parents. They will work very hard to do things they know will gain the smiles, kisses and pats that go along with the approval of Mom and Dad. At young ages, kids will do things they have little or no interest in because they know they will gain favor with their parents.

With Keeping Kids Safe we bring parents into our classes, exercises and techniques. Why not have kids engage in safety activities that benefit them while they also receive approval and applause from their parents? It is called "Positive Feedback" and we use it all the time. It is the most effective way we know to teach kids personal safety It simply accelerates the learning process for the child.

Positive reinforcement techniques are pretty simple. "Good job!" "That's super!" "Great! Next time let's see if we can do…" are all positive reinforcement words. Make sure there is enough "You're great!" added in there, too. Along with words make sure your body language says the same things: eye contact and full attention focused on your child when they are speaking to you.

Second, practice at home reinforces safety issues through repetition. We are great believers in repetition. It is the most time honored teaching tool on the planet and we use it relentlessly.

Repetition does not mean dull, either. It simply means doing things again and again. There are many ways we repeat things so kids remember however they are carefully disguised as fun and new and exciting for kids. We come at our safety ideas from many different angles in our classes for the express purpose of keeping things interesting for the children and parents alike. It is just flat out true, that the more kids are exposed to something, the better they learn it. If your child grows weary of hearing an idea repeatedly, be thankful. That means they have learned it so well that it now bores them a bit. This is far better than them being exposed to an idea only once in class and not have it take root in their memory. Parents must take our ideas out of the classroom and use them at home for the safest kids.

The Philosophy Of Safety

We also know kids learn by watching. Who do kids watch the most? Who do kids get influenced the most by when they are young? The answer is their parents.

It does not matter if the behavior is positive or negative, the child observes, the child mimics, the behavior of their most cherished icons, Mom and Dad. Kids watch and learn from the examples set by their parents. This is why parents can capitalize on teaching their children silently by example, by being the best they can be as adults.

"By being the best they can be as adults and as parents." Are you?

To get the most out of teaching your child to keep themselves safe, you need to be the best you can be as an adult and set that example. Are you a confident person? Are you calm in a crisis? Do you have a positive outlook and "can do attitude?"

These are critical qualities your child needs to have in order to be able to keep themselves safe when you are not around. The are critical qualities you need to display for them to learn as they watch you go through life. Do you have them?

Whether you want to be or not, whether you consciously work at it or not, whether you believe this or not, your child is watching, absorbing and mimicking very quietly everything about you as their parent.

So, Mom and Dad, you need to be the best you can be.

Setting The Example

So how do you do any of this with kids, family, jobs, obligations and just flat out the every day demands of living in today's world?

There are two simple steps. One, start. Yes. Take action and just start somewhere rather than debate, think and plan. Take action and just start doing any one idea we have in this book.

If you do one thing every other day for a few weeks it will open doors that will bring you ideas and ways to move and improve.

It can be as simple as telling your child how good they are. Then, tell yourself how good a person you are, too! Then follow up with telling yourself you feel good. Every day, whether you do or not, tell yourself you feel good. Every day, several times a day say to yourself, "I feel Good!" Say it with meaning, say it with emotion, and say it often.

Two, even if you do not feel good, say it! Delete the negative thoughts. Just STOP them in your mind. Focus on feeling good. It will take hold after a relatively short period of time.

You may think this is silly but feeling good is the foundation for all good things that are to follow.

Did you know your kids do this unconsciously? Their first thought in the morning is not "OOOO! My Back!" Kids think about their toys, what they want to eat and where they are going for the day that will be fun and make them feel good.

As adults we learned day after day, over the years, how not to feel good. Remember those times as a child when you felt great? GO back to remembering those days if you have to do so. Be like a child in your mind. Be like your child. Train your mind to feel good.

What did you dream about at 8 years old? Watch your kids as they play. They have wild facial expressions and their words come out with giddy laughs. Eyes are wide as they talk about fun things. Kids dream about and play at being great people when they grow up. They imitate their heroes and people that impress them.

Every answer to "what do you want to grow up to be?" is accompanied by waving hands and full body gesture as they see in their minds eye what they are thinking. We hear kid's dreams about being happy, doing fun things, being a famous dancer, astronaut, scientist, explorer or symphony musician.

We never once heard a child say that they want to have a dead end job and surround themselves with debt, stress, worry or money problems.

You should be who your child wants to be. You should be someone your child looks up to an wants to imitate. Make it a positive image for them.

Somewhere along the way of growing up most adults let go of their dreams. In letting go of them, most adults also lose the desire to continually move forward and evolve as human beings.

We think life can be better the older you get. We know life is better the older you get. Improving, moving forward, evolution, growth, what ever it is you call it you can do it and strive for your dreams what ever your age.

Dreams are for adults.

Find your dreams again. Sure, they've changed since your were a child. Maybe they have not. Spend some quiet time resurfacing your dreams again.

It may seam like a child's fantasy and that is the point. Become more child-like. Kids hold onto their dreams because they have not been conditioned to let go of them. The negative influences of our society drum us into submission to let go and become one of the masses.

It is never too late to find a dream and pursue it. It will keep you young and keep you excited for the rest of your life. It will make a difference with you and your child. It could even help make your child safer when their Mom and Dad is the best they can be.

The I Can Principle

We have two rules for the kids in our classes that we have mentioned before:

- Always Do Your Best

- Always Say "I can!"

These are perfect for parents to embrace for themselves, too.

I can.

When the child lives these ideas daily the learning is even faster. If parents live these principles and apply them to the family in general, they make better parents. They make better families.
How can you do this?

Start by saying daily "I can."

Saying, "I Can!" may seem silly at first, even if you don't feel that way. Stick with it. Your example will set the stage for your child better than you can possibly imagine. If you can, what do you think your child could do?

Think of it this way, the better you are the better your child will be in all areas of their life, safety included. Now do it. Say, I Can!" Commit to and do it several times a day.

Chapter Summary

There are certain Immutable Laws Of Safety to follow in order to insure that kids, who need to learn to keep themselves safe, understand and learn what we are teaching them.

- Law #1: Get Their Attention

- Law #2: Build Their Confidence

- Law #3: A Stranger Is Someone You Don't Know Very Well

- Law #4: It's "OK" To Talk To Strangers

- Law #5: When A Stranger Approaches Engage A Circle Of Safety

- Law #6: Speak In A Power Voice

- Law #7: Yell "FIRE!" When In A Dangerous Situation

- Law #8: Listen To Your Belly Brain

- Law# 9: When Grabbed By A Predator, Yell, Point and Look

- Ultimate safety comes from parents.

- Kids get the most out of what we teach them when we engage the parents as part of the teaching and learning process.

- Practice at home reinforces safety issues through repetition.

- Parents must take our ideas out of the classroom and use them at home for the safest kids.

- To get the most out of teaching your child to keep themselves safe, you need to be the best you can be as an adult and set that example.

- Every day, several times a day say to yourself, "I feel Good!" Say it with meaning, say it with emotion, and say it often.

- Two, even if you do not feel good, say it! Delete the negative thoughts.

- You should be who your child wants to imitate. Make it a positive image.

- Find your dreams again. It is never too late to find a dream and pursue it.

- Say daily to yourself, "I can."

- The better you are the better your child will be in all areas of their life, safety included.

5

MASTERING YOUR CHILD'S SAFETY

The Magic In Simplicity

Our approach to child safety, our entire Keeping Kids Safe program for that matter, is "Simplicity By Design." Simplicity creates magical results with kids in our classes.

The beauty of it is in our approach is in its simplicity and it is intentional. We take complex subjects like child safety, psychology, teaching techniques and parenting skills and blend them in such a way as to create a seamless and easy program that kids can learn and use on their own.

The easiest part in our approach is working with the kids themselves. As long as we keep our classes and information exciting and interesting, we can teach kids everything we need to teach them about keeping themselves safe. The difficult and challenging part can be in working with the parents.

Where Real Safety Begins

Real safety begins at home. Therefore, we have to work with the parents. In order to keep a child safe, the bottom line is that parents have to be on top of things as an adult and a parent, in order to reinforce what we teach, at home. Parents need to be solid, centered adults.

We find that many parents who come to our class are not on top of things. For all kinds of reasons, we as adults, carry around too much "baggage" in our lives. Memories, incidents, thoughts and feelings from the past, that subconsciously transfers to our children, bog down even the best parental intentions.

We also find many of the parents that bring their children to our classes are not particularly confident in themselves. We find many have lost their drive and desire for their dreams and goals in life. We find many are trapped in jobs they hate. Many feel overburdened, worried and tired.

As we've mentioned, parents need to teach, mentor and lead their children by example, both in life and safety.

Changing Your Destiny For Your Child

Therefore, we involve parents in everything we teach. We subtly, and sometimes not so subtly, fold Mom and Dad into every class. We work with the parents, too, so they can be their best. We improve families and kids together in order to keep them all safe.

Sometimes we work with parents as much as we work with some of the kids. The message is blunt but clear: take care of yourself in order to take care of your kids. Be the best you can be so your child is the best they can be.

If not, then we try to help them understand they need to change, they need to improve. We help them commit to self improvement and they learn along with their child.

We talk to parents about having the ability to take action. Action is required in improving themselves and in teaching their children great safety for a lifetime.   Parents must take action and be capable of change for their children's sake.

If a parent does not want to hear our message or cannot change when it is required, then they can forget about helping their kids. It's painful but it's the brutal truth.

To all parents we say, we can help you!

Every single one of our classes ties into better parenting skills. If you have good skills we'll help you make them better. If you need to learn better skills we'll teach them to you. Most parents will do it because it's about their kid's safety. It's about being the best you can be as an individual and adult and parent role model for your kids.

Be warned that some of the information we have will make you uncomfortable. Some of the ideas we teach are controversial. But everything we teach we stand behind and it works. Keeping Kids Safe is controversial but it is also effective.

The bottom line is, how much do you want to be a little less worried about your kids when you are not around? If you ever stayed awake at night worrying about your kids than this is for you and your family.

Why? Because Keeping Kids Safe is our business.

Safety, even Keeping Kids Safe safety, depends on parents teaching, nurturing, embracing and reinforcing our ideas and techniques with their kids.

For the last twenty years we have been developing and teaching the Keeping Kids Safe program. It is a great child safety program.

In Walnut Creek, California we "home base" with a series of 10 week Keeping Kids Safe classes throughout the year. These are open to anyone who cares about children and their safety.

The Proven Success Formula For Safe Kids

Our proven success formula to stop sexual predators cold is simplicity itself, too. First, we teach kids to feel good about themselves. When they do, they start to be more confident.

We know confident kids stand a little taller, keep their shoulders back and their heads up little higher and are by nature, less of a target for sexual predators. We also know confident kids display certain physical structural changes that allow them to better control their body movements. We see enhanced mental focus and concentration. These two characteristics add up to making the Keeping Kids Safe safety techniques that much more effective.

Our proven success formula to stop sexual predators cold is simplicity itself, too. First, we teach kids to feel good about themselves. Then, we teach parents how to build on this at home. When they both understand what we are doing, we can then teach them both real, effective safety techniques.

Through a series of fun games in the form of cleverly disguised repetition exercises, kids that do not know what it's like to feel confident down to their very core begin to experience the feelings of it. While it is sad but true, there really are some children today that do not regularly experience praise and positive reinforcement enough to build confidence. We help them.

For the child that already displays confidence, we simply build on it. They begin to learn others see them in a good way and they will begin to understand they can find people in the world to be around like that by choice.

At the same time, we show Mom and Dad some of our skills so they can reinforce these good feelings and nurture confidence at home. From simple good feelings come the roots of real confidence and this must take hold at home.

In the Appendix of this book we've outlined some of our fun games we play in teaching kids safety. Flip over to check it out and enjoy playing them with your child.

Serious Fun For Safer Kids

We take information, even on a subject as serious as child safety, and make it fun to learn. Kids learn best when they have fun doing so.

We teach in a way that makes each class fun for your child by using language they use. We sequence information in ways we know kids will absorb it and retain it.

We start by introducing concepts and certain terms in the first few weeks to both parents and kids. We subtly weave these concepts together with a series of fun exercises and exciting games that aid and reinforce the learning process with kids.

While we teach the children themselves we work with the families as a total unit. We have a secondary focus to make families and everyone in it better by learning and practicing safety as a family.

Chapter Summary

- Our approach to child safety, our entire Keeping Kids Safe program for that matter, is "Simplicity By Design."

- Simplicity creates magical results with kids in our classes.

- We take complex subjects like child safety, psychology, teaching techniques and parenting skills and blend them in such a way as to create a seamless and easy program that kids can learn and use on their own.

- Real safety begins at home.

- We involve parents in everything we teach.

- Every single one of our classes ties into better parenting skills. and your family.

- Why? Because Keeping Kids Safe is our business.

- Safety, even Keeping Kids Safe safety, depends on parents teaching, nurturing, embracing and reinforcing our ideas and techniques with their kids.

- Our proven success formula to stop sexual predators cold is simplicity itself, too. First, we teach kids to feel good about themselves. Then, we teach parents how to build on this at home. When they both understand what we are doing, we can then teach them both real, effective safety techniques through a series of fun games. Check out the Safety Games in the Appendix of this book.

- We take information, even on a subject as serious as child safety, and make it fun to learn.

6

ONLINE SEXUAL PREDATORS

The 10 Secrets To Stopping Online Predators Cold!

Ah! The Internet. The wonderful World Wide Web. A whole new door of information and possibilities has opened in our lifetimes. And, it is still in its infancy. It is expanding everyday. By the time our children are grown, some estimates project the Internet will be ten times larger and more expansive than it is today.

This highlights a macabre nightmare opening of a web based Pandora's Box for any parent today. The "Information Highway" is loaded with danger for kids, and kids of several age groups.

It is impossible to stop all the sexual predators online. Our approach is to arm you with our best information so you can stay one step ahead of these derelict individuals.

The Sly Disguises Of Online Sexual Predators

First, it is important to understand just how the Internet is used by predators. They use it to troll for unsuspecting children in a number of ways. Some predators like to befriend a child first. Often, this process involves lots of attention, kindness and even gifts offered by the predator to the child. This type of sexual predator is very, very patient and will take the time to allow the trap to develop over time. The process will also slowly introduce sexual context and content into conversations and communications.

Some predators immediately engage in sexually explicit conversations with children. Still others collect and trade child-pornographic images, while others seek real face to face meetings with kids. Regardless of the approach, it is important to know that the FBI states that there is no one profile for an online sexual predator. They can be any age or sex. There is no one profile. Teenagers are particularly targeted because of their natural curiosity in sex due to their growing sexual nature. Online sexual predators exploit this.

Second, the ease of access to the Internet attracts predators, too. Cars, gasoline, security cameras and witnesses are just some of the things that predators eliminate in their stalking of victims.

Third, the Internet affords a layer of anonymity that offline or direct sexual predators do not have. Anyone online can easily hide behind a user name and prowl websites and social networks with a free email account.

The Warning Signs You Must Know That Your Child Is In Danger From An Online Predator

One of the warning signs your child may be in the throes of being victimized online is that they may become withdrawn from the family. Online predators will work very hard at driving a wedge between a child and their family. One way they do this is by accentuating any minor problems at home that your child might have. The predator poses as an understanding friend and drives a wedge into the family structure.

The number one warning sign that your child might be involved with an online predator is with your child withdrawing from the family. It is not always the reason children withdraw but it can be an indication of contact with sexual predators.

Some other warning signs would be if your child displays anxious behavior about going to a particular place or seeing a person. Your child may suddenly have behavior problems such as aggressiveness or extreme mood swings such as brooding, crying or fearfulness. Their grades may take a nosedive precipitously.

The Dangers Of Social Networks And Blogs

We all have seen the headlines in the news. Predators have met victims who met on Social Networks or Blogs such as MySpace, Friendster, Xanga, and Facebook. These sites are where people can meet, communicate, and interact with each other online.

They are very popular and memberships are exploding in growth. Anyone who can get online can join and start interacting with each other immediately. CNN reports the number of visitors to MySpace went from 4.9 million in 2005 to currently over 67 million in 2006. A report from October 2006 had it at 243% growth. Recent reports in 2007 show similar gains in visitors.

It's not just MySpace. Social networking sites are popping up weekly fueled by the speculation of their market value to advertisers.

We do want to state that most activity within these networks and blogs is legal and positive. The best way to insure safety for your child, if they visit these sites, is a few simple rules set up by you, Mom and Dad.

First, many kids are not aware they are putting themselves in danger by giving out too much personal information and communicating with people they've only met online. These problems get larger because most kids, especially teenagers, do not inform their parents of online incidents.

The 10 Secrets For Internet Safety Today

Why would you, Mom and Dad, be the starting point of a safety program that helps you keep your kids safe from sexual predators? It is because you, as a parent, are integral in keeping your kids safe. Not only that, you are the centerpiece in teaching them to keep themselves safe.

Secret #1: Know The Websites Your Child Visits

You're in charge, Mom and Dad. Monitor your child when they are online. Sit with them while they surf and play. If you do not sit with them while they are online and your child is pre-teen, consider installing available filters that let you control the sites they can visit. It is not about mistrust, it's about knowledge. Preteens can accidentally visit a porn site where "cookies" are surreptitiously deposited on your computer. This typically opens the door for SPAM and more unwanted intrusions into your life.

Secret #2: Set Up Rules For Your Child Online

Decide on the time of day, length of time and websites that your child can visit.

Secret #3: Teach Your Child Not To Give Out Any Personal Information Online

Teach your child to treat online contacts just like the strangers they are. Personal information is none of their business! This includes telephone number, address, parents' work address and telephone number and the name and location of schools.

Secret #4: Make An Agreement With Your Child That They Will Come To You If They Come Across Anything Online That Makes Them Uncomfortable

With this agreement you must make sure you stay calm, open and listen without judgment when they come to you. This goes back to trust and listening skills and cannot be emphasized enough as important in your child's safety. This also goes back to strong families. Your child must feel comfortable and confident in being able to come to you with anything.

Secret #5: Do Not Allow Your Child To Agree To Meet Anyone In Person They Met Online

If your child wants to meet someone, make sure you go with them and you set up the meeting in a public place. Make sure you view all correspondence that your child has created prior to agreeing to this type of meeting.

Secret #6: Never let Your Child Upload A Picture Of Themselves to the Internet

There is no reason today for a picture of your child to be posted on the web for any reason without your permission. This way, they do not have the ability to send it to anyone. If there really is a need for a photo online of your child, make sure you review the reasons why and carefully weigh the options.

Secret #7: Teach Your Child To Ignore Any Email Messages That are Uncomfortable To Read Or Mean In Spirit

"CyberBullying" is a problem as well as sexually explicit material. Both have negative consequences for your child and need to be ignored and filtered.

Secret #8: Teach Your Child Never To Give Out Their Password To Anyone

Emphasize with your child that this means their best friends, too. Parents are the only ones that should know their child's passwords. Make sure you have them written down somewhere.

Secret #9: Never Let Your Child Download Software Without Your Permission

Make sure nothing gets put onto your computer unless you know about it. This includes games, programs and other materials that could include hidden items that jeopardize your family's privacy.

Secret #10: Take Immediate Action If You Suspect Your Child Has Been Contacted by A Sexual Predator

Take immediate action. Never sit around to wait to see if a situation is threatening or will develop. There are several good cyber reporting agencies that can help you. See the Appendix in this book for help.

Chapter Summary.

- It is impossible to stop all the sexual predators online. Our approach is to arm you with our best information so you can stay one step ahead of these derelict individuals.

- It is important to understand just how the Internet is used by predators.

- One of the warning signs your child may be in the throes of being victimized online is that they may become withdrawn from the family.

- Online predators will work very hard at driving a wedge between a child and their family.

- Some other warning signs would be if your child displays anxious behavior about going to a particular place or seeing a person.

- Your child may suddenly have behavior problems such as aggressiveness or extreme mood swings such as brooding, crying or fearfulness. Their grades may take a nosedive precipitously.

- Many kids are not aware they are putting themselves in danger by giving out too much personal information and communicating with people they've only met online.

- The 10 Secrets To Internet Safety

- Secret #1: Know The Websites Your Child Visits

- Secret #2: Set Up Rules For Your Child Online

- Secret #3: Teach Your Child Not To Give Out Any Personal Information Online

- Secret #4: Make An Agreement With Your Child That They Will Come To You If They Come Across Anything Online That Makes Them Uncomfortable

- Secret #5: Do Not Allow Your Child To Agree To Meet Anyone In Person They Met Online

- Secret #6: Never let Your Child Upload A Picture Of Themselves to the Internet

- Secret #7: Teach Your Child To Ignore Any Email Messages That are Uncomfortable To Read Or Mean In Spirit

- Secret #8: Teach Your Child Never To Give Out Their Password To Anyone

- Secret #9: Never Let Your Child Download Software Without Your Permission

- Secret #10: Take Immediate Action If You Suspect Your Child Has Been Contacted by A Sexual Predator

7

OFFLINE OR DIRECT CONTACT SEXUAL PREDATORS

Threats In Our Very Neighborhoods

When your child goes out of your home they are in the realm of offline or direct sexual predators. In your neighborhood, at your parks, on your streets and outside the fences of your schools, direct sexual predators are surreptitiously hunting for children. You can choose to spend every second supervising your child between birth and high school. How practical is that? How much does that instill in your child personal responsibility and growth? There is a better way.

These predators are hard to spot because they look like normal individuals. Your child can encounter threatening situations simply by playing in your yard with you in the house. The best way to protect your child is to teach them how to be able to keep themselves safe.

Step one is for your child to be able to know how to deal with strangers and how to deal effectively with them when approached by one. Your child must be able to respond and stay away from developing dangerous situations as well as getting out of one if caught in it. They must also be able to stay calm, focus and apply any number of safety techniques if a situation rapidly gets out of control.

We have Five Secrets for playing outside that you can teach your child. They can use them immediately and be a little safer when you are not around. They apply to any outdoor situation including times, like at the park, when you are close but not directly next to your child.

The 5 Secrets For Playing Safely Outside

Secret #1: Teach Your Child To Pay Attention To Things That Seem Out Of Place

Teach your child to be on the look out for things that occur that are out of the ordinary. Tell them it is "OK" for them to come tell you when they see something different. Say it and mean it. It does not matter what it is, just get them in the bait of telling you about things they see that just don't seem normal to them.

Things out of the ordinary are things like people moving through your neighborhood that are not normally there, cars moving much more slowly up and down your street than usual, vehicles repeatedly driving up and down your street or an unrecognizable ice cream truck appearing out of nowhere one afternoon.

Secret #2: Teach Your Child How To Sit Properly When Playing

Sitting properly means your child has their back is straight, head high and shoulders straight even when they are looking around or down. Show your child how to sit and play with their legs crossed and back straight. Sitting on their knees or with them bent to the side is also very effective for quick movement as long as their back is straight.

This sitting posture allows your child the ability to spot things out of the ordinary and gives them an advantage if they need to stand up quickly.

Teach your child this new sitting posture with a series of really fun games. Call them silly titles like the "Super Hero Sitting Game" or the "Who Can Sit The Longest Game" or even "I Can Sit Taller Than You Game." Whatever you call it, make it exciting for your child so you have and can hold their attention.

Start by having them sit on the floor and remind them "Back Straight!" and "Head Up!" Have them move around and do different things while on the floor. At random intervals call out "Power Seat!" and have them quickly move back into the starting position with back straight and head up. Correct any slouching with "Back Straight!" and "Head Up!"

Let the giggles roll as you play this game. Gently correct bad postures with positive words and guidance. Play the games with 15 to 20 second sitting intervals at a time and increase it as your child learns to be more comfortable in this sitting posture. Be creative in the game and add your own ideas.

Secret #3: Teach Your Child To Get To Their Feet Quickly And Tell You About Things That Are Not Normal

In a potential threatening situation a child needs to be able to get up fast and move quickly yet steadily. We teach kids to move fast and we teach them to do it under control. It starts with being able to get up properly off the ground. With good focus skills they can learn to do this easily and will be able to do it with a great deal of calm control.

The way most kids get up opens them up for being blindsided in an attack or abduction. Just watch your kids when they are watching TV. When they get up they usually stick their bum in the air first, put their hands on the ground and point their head down as they push themselves up with their arms. This method affords your child absolutely no protection or ability to see anything or anyone.

Teach them how to stand up so they can keep their heads up and eyes alert and up. This means they stand up without bending over and without placing their hands on the ground. They can do this by raising up to their knees first with head and shoulders straight, then placing a knee out at ninety degrees to their torso and then rotating up using the hips to a full standing position.

The end result is a child upright and alert with head up, shoulders back and ready to move quickly if required.

Again, teaching this technique to kids is done best with a fun game. Come up with a great name like "The Stand In A Flash Game" and offer a "win" reward at the end for your child when they move in a flash.

Even better, you can tie this game to the "Sitting Game" in the prior Secret. Have them sit properly with back straight and head up, then have them "jump up in a flash."

The fun can really roll and the learning take hold when your child jumps up fast, moves around, then sits down quickly and correctly.
Make sure each time you play this game you offer a little more of a challenge or contest, possibly reward, as they increase their skills.

Secret #4: Teach Your Child To Look People, Especially Adults, Directly In The Eyes

Teach your child to look at people directly in the eyes, especially adults. Kids need to learn to look adults directly in the eyes. Very few children look adults right in the eyes when they are talking to them. Kids are naturally intimidated by adults because we are bigger and stronger than they are. It is just a natural thing, but you can teach your child to have the confidence to look anyone in the eyes.

Looking someone in the eyes does many things for a child. One, it projects confidence that anyone approaching the child can see. Two, it allows the child some time to assess the intentions of the approaching individual. Three, a small child squarely and confidently looking at an approaching stranger in the eyes, can give the child an extra split second advantage in fleeing a dangerous situation if that stranger is taken by surprise with the intense gaze of that small child.

Secret #5: Teach Your Child To Listen To Their Instincts

Another tool your child's safety arsenal is teaching them that they have two brains, the one in their head and one in their belly. We call the one in the belly the "Belly Brain." Adults know this as their "gut instinct."

Kids need to learn to listen to their Belly Brain. It is rarely, if ever, wrong. Kids have this gut feeling too, but they need some help in learning how to listen to it and use it to keep themselves safe.

Teach your child that the Belly Brain works for them. Teach them how to listen to it. Help your child to distinguish between their "Head Brain" and their Belly Brain.

In our classes we show the kids how their Head Brain can sometimes trick them. We use imagination and storytelling techniques that enable the children to build up a great, exciting tale about a shadow they saw dance across a wall. It's the same when kids think monsters are in their bedroom closet or under the bed. We show them how their Head Brain makes these stories up.

Reinforce the Belly Brain as the alarm clock for potentially dangerous situations. Teach your child to trust and always listen to it at all times. You can show your kids how to recognize the uneasiness in their stomach without panic, alarm and worry. When kids tune into their Belly Brain they are more tuned in detecting uncomfortable situations, situations with questionable adults and inappropriate behavior.

Kids naturally feel uncomfortable with inappropriate questions and behaviors they are around. We simply show them how to be alert to it with their Belly Brain.

Security In Neighborhood Safety Clubs

Our goal is to help you thwart sexual predators that prowl your neighborhood. One way is to set up alternate "safe" areas with your trusted neighbors. Some of our Keeping Kids Safe families have set up their own neighborhood safety clubs just for this purpose.

Give your children more than one safe
haven if outside when a predator shows up.
Not only should your child look for you
first, they should have an alternate place to
go in the event their path to you is cut off by
the predator.

Set up procedures to alert you if they wind
up in their alternate place. Whether you live
in an apartment, condominium or
neighborhood with single family homes, set
up a safety option with your child.

Walk them through the alternate areas.
Show them who to seek out and what to do
once they get there. Set up your own club to
help stop predators cold.

Chapter Summary

- Teach your child to be able to deal with strangers and how to deal effectively with them when approached by one.

- Your child must be able to respond and stay away from developing dangerous situations as well as getting out of one if caught in it.

- They must also be able to stay calm, focus and apply any number of safety techniques if a situation rapidly gets out of control.

- We have Five Secrets for playing outside that you can teach your child:

- Secret #1: Teach Your Child To Pay Attention To Things That Seem Out Of Place

- Secret #2: Teach Your Child How To Sit Properly When Playing

- Secret #3: Teach Your Child To Get To Their Feet Quickly And Tell You About Things That Are Not Normal

- Secret #4: Teach Your Child To Look People, Especially Adults, Directly In The Eyes

- Secret #5: Teach Your Child To Listen To Their Instincts

- Give your children more than one safe haven if outside when a predator shows up.

- Set up procedures to alert you if they wind up in their alternate place.

8

TOTAL SAFETY

The Amazing Secrets To Keeping Kids Safe

We want to give you a complete picture of our Keeping Kids Safe program. There are a lot of ideas and safety techniques presented in this book. Now we will show you how we use it ourselves, step by step, in our 10 week classroom course.

Since our program is about kids and their ability to keep themselves safe, our focus is on each child that comes through the door of our classroom.

From the time they step through that door, we call every child a Super Hero. We use this tag over 10 weeks with great emphasis. It helps us get the results we need. It is a teaching tool.

Why?

Super Heroes, for both boys and girls are still fun. Fun gets kids attention. Super Heroes are cartoon characters that can do and be anything. Whether it is Superman or Wonder Woman, Luke Skywalker, Ariel, or Snow White, these characters perform magical feats that kids can relate to and understand. This analogy is the key in having the kids in our classes think they can do everything we teach them. So they become Super Heroes.

Using Super Heroes as examples is an attention getting gimmick that gets us the results we want in teaching kids to keep themselves safe. It is not rocket science but it is smart, effective teaching. We capitalize and constantly emphasize the Super Hero traits we want kids to learn: feeling strong, feeling confident, moving in a flash, using a power voice and super vision along with super mental focus skills.

Not only do we introduce Super Heroes, we continue each week building on those special Super Hero super traits. Without the kids knowing it, we are quietly arming them with personal safety arsenal of techniques. Then, in the final weeks we pull it all together for the kids and their parents with comprehensive exercises and play acting. We call them Super Hero Games.

So, what do we teach the kids and how does this work? We teach the kids to move fast and we teach them to do it under control. In a potential threatening situation a child needs to be able to move quickly yet steadily.

We also show them how to "Sit Like A Super Hero." This means sitting down with legs crossed, hands on their knees, back straight, head high, shoulder square and eyes forward.

Then we show them how to "Stand Like A Super Hero." This means to stand up without bending over and without placing their hands on the ground. The idea is to stand up with the head up and eyes forward. They do this by placing a knee out at ninety degrees and then rotating up using the hips. The end result is a child upright and alert with head up, shoulders back and ready to move again quickly if required.

Now, for the games! True learning comes with repetition. Repetition for kids is boring so we make repetitive actions into games they can play. We have lots of fun and laughter playing the "Up And Down Game."

It reinforces quick, correct movement and mental focus with a series of commands of "Everybody Up!" and "Everybody Down!" A contest or two to see who is the fastest adds to the fun and excitement of the game.

When in a potentially dangerous situation, and your child may be caught unaware, they need to be able to move quickly while they keep an eye on the developing situation. If a sexual predator approaches them, your child needs to get up quickly, keep an eye on the approaching individual and leave the area fast and safely.

The Power Of Focus

Teaching kids to move quickly, yet in a fun manner, will teach them to be safer. It also leads into the next safety technique. After a few practice sessions in moving like a Super Hero the children in our classes are ready to learn how to sharpen their mental focus skills to a higher degree.

We teach children as young as four to mentally focus and concentrate. This is paramount in teaching your child to keep themselves safe. The fact is, if your child cannot focus, they will never be able to keep themselves safe. It is so critical and important to child safety we call it the Power Of Focus.

Whenever a threatening situation is developing your child needs to be able to spot it. When they spot it they must focus on it to see the danger and get away from it before it develops and engulfs them. So, we teach the children in our classes to focus. If a child needs to learn this skill, we teach them If a child already has this skill, we improve it.

We start with our command of "Sit Like A Super Hero!" And reinforce "Back straight!" then, "Eyes Forward!" We ask the kids to pick one spot in front of them and look only at that one spot. Starting with 15 to 20 seconds at a time we do this as a game and watch for wandering eyes. We correct them with, "Eyes Forward! Focus!"

The fun really starts as we have the kids jump up like a Super Hero, move around, then "Sit Like A Super Hero!" with a following command of "Focus!" Each time they sit, the following focusing exercise becomes a little longer. Over time, most kids can sit for one to two minutes or more and focus at will. They can turn it on and off at their choosing.

When they really get good with this we offer a little game, a challenge and contest to see who can sit and focus the longest. Again, we must constantly play games and have fun as we build skills and better mental focus.

Mental focus, what we call the Power Of Focus, is built, practiced and reinforced in every class in some fashion because of the critical nature of it in real child safety.

It is worth saying again:

A CHILD'S ABILITY TO ASSESS A POTENTIAL DANGEROUS SITUATION DEVELOPING OR ONE THEY MUST GET AWAY FROM DEPENDS ON THEIR ABILITY TO MENTALLY FOCUS

The Secret To A Better Family

Better mental focus in a child is also one of the huge benefits of our Keeping Kids Safe program that translates directly to better families.

When your child can focus better you can talk or communicate with them more easily and get better results from them. Better focus means they will look at you when you speak to them and respond to you more quickly and easily.

It's True! Try it. We actually do these exercises in class to show both parents and children how it works. One, it reinforces our safety lessons and two, it does make family life better.

Do this:

1. Have the child sit Like A Super Hero
   - Back straight
   - Legs crossed
   - Hands on knees
   - Eyes forward

2. Get down on the floor and look into their eyes
   - Ask them to look directly at you

3. Ask your child clearly, calmly and succinctly to do what you want them to do
   - For example, pick up their shoes in the middle of the floor and place them neatly by the door

The results speak for themselves. Whether it's cleaning their room, picking up their shoes or sitting at the dinner table, we get parents into the habit of talking to their kids on important matters in this manner.

Penetrating Laser Eyes

Very few children look people in the eyes, especially people they are talking to. Very few kids look adults right in the eyes for any reason. Kids are naturally intimidated by larger, older adults.

We teach kids in our classes to look anyone they talk to, even adults, right in the eyes. It is a skill kids need to learn. When we teach them this skill we call it using Super Hero Laser Eyes.

This skill also helps enhance mental focus in children. When a child is confronted with danger from another individual, they need to be able to look that person in the eyes when they respond.

Looking someone in the eyes does many things for a child. One, it projects confidence that anyone approaching the child can see. Two, it allows the child to clearly assess the intentions of the approaching individual. Three, it gives your child the ability to figure out a safe route out. Four, in some cases a small child squarely and confidently looking at an approaching stranger in the eyes can give the child an extra split second advantage in fleeing a dangerous situation when that stranger is taken by surprise with the intense gaze of that small child.

Super Hero Power Voice

Another technique we layer into our safety techniques is a "Super Hero Power Voice." This teaches a child to use a strong voice that comes from the abdomen, not the throat. Each child is capable of this type of voice although they may not have ever used it or know they even have it.

When kids yell, and most adults too, they yell from their throat. The Super Hero Power Voice is a yell from their belly.

Put your hand on your abdomen and push out with your stomach muscles. Do it again and huff out a breath with it. Do it one more time and this time push out your breath and make a sound with it.

It sounds like a deep "Huh!" More importantly, it comes out with a measure of strength and power. This is the kids' Super Hero Power Voice.

We practice this by telling the children to, "Bounce Your Voice off The Walls!" Again, it comes from the abdomen, not the throat and when done correctly the difference is astonishing. Kids will need to learn this voice if they ever need to use it. It will get people's attention when it is used.

Super Hero Belly Brains

We teach kids they have two brains, the one in their head and one in their belly. We call the one in the belly the Super Hero Belly Brain.

Kids know how to listen to their Head Brain. They do it everyday, all the time. We teach kids the differences between their two brains and how to listen to their Belly Brain. We teach them their Belly Brain is always right.

For adults, a Belly Brain is that visceral, gut feeling that is always right. Kids have this gut feeling too, but they need some help in learning how to listen to it and use it to keep themselves safe.

We simply show kids how their Belly Brain works. We show them it is always right and always works positively for them. We teach them to pay attention to it and how to listen to it. More importantly, we show them that listening to it is "OK," as well.

In doing this we have to show the kids how their Head Brain can sometimes trick them. We do this by using imagination and storytelling techniques that enable the children to build up a great, exciting tale about a shadow they saw dance across a wall.

It's the same when kids think monsters that are in their bedroom closet or under the bed.

We show them how their Head Brain makes these stories up.

We then reinforce the Belly Brain as the alarm clock for potentially dangerous situations. We teach the kids to recognize the uneasiness in their stomach without panic, alarm and worry. We teach them to see potential danger calmly and avoid it with any number of ways we teach.

When kids tune into their Belly Brain they are more tuned in detecting uncomfortable situations, situations with questionable adults and inappropriate behavior. Kids naturally feel uncomfortable with inappropriate questions and behaviors they are around. We simply show them how to be alert to it with their Super Hero Belly Brain.

The kids learn not only to listen to their Belly Brain but to also go tell Mom and Dad about how they feel and who they were with when they tune into it.

The Best Circle Of Safety

Now that many of the kids are armed with a lot of the Super Hero traits we want them to have, like confidence, focus, quick movement and two brains, we subtly begin to weave them into actual situations where kids can use them to keep themselves safe.

At this point we can start to teach actual safety techniques. A good technique to start with is what to do with approaching strangers. When a stranger approaches, any stranger by our Keeping Kids Safe definition, we teach the kids to use a Circle Of Safety.

A Circle of Safety in a child safety program is not a new idea. Many programs teach this technique. They teach a Circle of Safety of about 8' to 10' circling a child in the middle of it. The child does not allow anyone to enter the circle without them turning and running to safety.

The Circle of Safety is a pretty easy idea to teach kids, too. This basic Circle Of Safety is a good idea in theory. It is true as long as no one moves.

This is the problem with most child safety programs that teach a Circle of Safety. In situations where kids are grabbed by predators, no one is standing still. At Keeping Kids Safe we take the idea of the Circle of Safety one giant step further. We teach a 15' to 20' Circle Of Safety.

Why? It's pretty simple: the standard 8' to 10' Circle Of Safety does not work if an adult blitzes in full speed to grab a kid. Kids need time to react and run at kid speed and still stay ahead of a running adult. The 8' to 10' circle does not give them enough reaction time.

We practice a Circle Of Safety with adults charging at the kids. What we find is the larger circle provides enough distance for even the smallest child to recognize what is happening, turn and run, and evade the grasp of a charging adult.

Kids need all the extra help they can when threatened and this larger circle gives them that extra bit.

Where does the child run? We teach them to run and look for someone they can trust:

- A parent
- An adult they know
- A police officer
- A firefighter
- A Mom with children

If the child is in a store or public place and is lost, we teach them to look for a woman with children, a Mom, for help. Chances are women with children are Moms and will more often help a child lost or in danger than other individuals.

When a child learns what a Circle Of Safety is, we teach them how to use it. How to use a Circle of Safety is just as important as knowing what it is. Kids at Keeping Kids Safe use a Circle of Safety to their advantage with their power voice and a simple command:

STOP! I'M NOT SUPPOSE TO GET CLOSE TO STRANGERS!

A Circle of Safety by itself is a good thing to teach children. To start, a child needs to see a stranger approaching them. Remember, a stranger is simply someone the child does not know very well. "Good" or "Bad" is irrelevant. A stranger, all strangers are dealt with in one, simple, easy way with Keeping Kids Safe.

As a stranger gets to the edge of their Circle Of Safety, we teach kids to raise their hand in a "halt" gesture and in their Super Hero Voice say, **"STOP!"**

The adult or approaching stranger will usually stop and ask, "Why?"

The child then says, "I'm not allowed to get close to strangers," again in their strong Super Hero Voice.

If the stranger continues toward the child, they have learned to turn and run away to someone for help.

If the stranger simply has a question like, "I'm looking for the hospital" they can still

ask the child from a distance. The 15' to 20'
Circle Of Safety allows for normal
conversation.

Good strangers can also recognize what the
child is doing and move away, again as most
responsible people will do, when this
happens.
Kids are taught in Keeping Kids Safe to
never let **ANY STRANGER** in their Circle
of Safety. If it happens then we teach them
to turn and run. A stranger, any stranger, is
to be dealt with in this straight forward,
simple manner, by kids.

When a child turns and runs from their
Circle Of Safety they need to get the
attention of someone that will help them
immediately.

We teach them to yell **"FIRE!"** whenever
they get into trouble.

Fire?! Yes, **"FIRE!"** for many reasons.

One, kids are always yelling when they play.
One of their favorite things to yell when
playing is "Help!"

They also tend to yell "Help!" in very high
pitched, throaty voices. Adults and other
family members quickly learn to ignore
these yells of "Help!"

If a child yells "Help!" and really means it, chances are they will be ignored. They will not get the help they need when they need it.

We teach kids to yell, **"FIRE!"** when they are in need of real help. The word "Fire!" gets anyone's attention immediately. Even if it is yelled in a high pitched throaty voice it will get people's attention.

The ideas behind these simple yet effective techniques to have one, simple rule kids, even the youngest kids, can do. That, is, kids are to keep a Circle Of Safety around themselves with any stranger. When a bad stranger invades the Circle Of Safety, a child is to turn and run while they yell "FIRE!" for help.

Chapter Summary

- From the time they step through that door, we call every child a Super Hero. It is a teaching tool.

- Using Super Heroes as examples is an attention getting gimmick that gets us the results we want in teaching kids to keep themselves safe.

- We teach kids how to "Sit Like A Super Hero.

- We teach kids how to "Stand Like A Super Hero."

- We teach kids how to use a "Super Hero Power Voice."

- We teach kids to listen to their "Super Hero Belly Brain."

- We teach kids how to use an expanded "Circle Of Safety."

- We teach kids how to yell "Fire!" when they are in trouble.

- We teach kids how to deal with strangers, any stranger, for total safety.

- We play games with the kids in our classes to reinforce the safety techniques we teach them.

- When in a potentially dangerous situation, and your child may be caught unaware, they need to be able to move quickly while they keep an eye on the developing situation. If a sexual predator approaches them, your child needs to get up quickly, keep an eye on the approaching individual and leave the area fast and safely.

- A child's ability to assess a potential dangerous situation developing or one they must get away from depends on their ability to mentally focus.

- Better mental focus in a child is also one of the huge benefits of our Keeping Kids Safe program that translates directly to better families.

- If the child is in a store or public place and is lost, we teach them to look for a woman with children, a Mom, for help.

9

PUTTING IT ALL
TOGETHER

More Secrets To Keeping
Kids Safe

What does teaching all these Super Hero traits to children mean? It means safer kids.

Here is how we put it all together at Keeping Kids Safe. Here is a quick summary of our philosophy, approach and techniques for kids being able to keep themselves safe.

First, your child should be able to be less of a target for predators and bullies by walking around looking more confident and happy, even when they don't necessarily feel that way.

With their shoulders back, head high and eyes alert to the environment around them, they do not make themselves appear to be an easy target when you are not around.

This means your child is becoming a Super Hero.

What happens if your child is sitting down, playing in a sand box at the playground and a bad stranger rapidly approaches them? It means your child can see them coming and get up quickly while keeping their eyes on the person.

This means your child is sitting like a Super Hero.

If you child is walking home from school with their head held high and tuned into their environment with sharp mental focus they should be able to see a potentially dangerous situation and avoid it.

This means your child is using Super Hero Eyes and Mentally Focusing.

If your child cannot consciously understand what is wrong but feels uneasy around a certain adult, they can leave the area and tell you about it. They are listening to their

Belly Brains and following their natural instincts to safety.

If a stranger approaches your child they engage a Circle Of Safety.

If a stranger gets too close to that Circle of Safety they command "STOP! I'm not suppose to get close to Strangers!" in their best voice from the abdomen.

If a child needs to turn and run and yell "FIRE!" with that abdominal voice they can get help quickly as they will be noticed.

This means your child is using their Super Hero Voice.

Mental focus, staying calm yet moving quickly to avoid a running stranger is all about what we teach at Keeping Kids Safe.

It means you child knows to find a police officer, fire fighter or Mother with other children if they ever get separated from you in a shopping mall or store.

It means that in many situations your child will be calm, in control and able to make good, solid choices for themselves quickly in order to get safe and stay safe.

It means, that while you are a parent that will always worry and care about your child, you will be able to worry just a little bit less than you did the day before.

More Secrets To Keep Your Kids Safe

What we have shared in this book is just a part of what we teach at Keeping Kids Safe. These are the basics of our philosophy and actual safety techniques.

Anyone at home committed to keeping their kids safe and being the best they can be can learn them and apply them.

In our classes we go further and add a few more techniques and things for kids to learn, especially in the horrible event they are grabbed by a bad stranger.

At Keeping Kids Safe we have developed **9 Easy GETAWAYS** that allow any child, your child, to be able to escape the grasp of any adult.

Here, we can describe them and give you an awareness of the tools which we can teach kids in order for them to keep themselves safe.

These **9 Easy GETAWAYS** are effective, even for very small and very young children. They are effective because the children learned how to focus, stay calm, and move quickly and in a controlled manner.

Children as young as four years old can implement them and use them effectively against larger, stronger adults. Yes, children are able to learn easily and remember all nine of the techniques.

Each of the **9 Easy GETAWAYS** is based upon principles of leverage, martial arts and training we have learned and tested over thirty years.

We have a Super Hero Voice yell that we teach the kids to use whenever they are grabbed. This yell mentally and physically prepares the child for the **9 Easy GETAWAYS** technique in addition to drawing immediate attention and help to them.

When a child is grabbed we teach them to yell:

FIRE! FIRE! HE'S NOT MY DAD!

The child looks directly into the grabbers eyes and points at them with their free hand while yelling.

The yell changes based upon who is grabbing. For an adult woman:

FIRE! FIRE! SHE'S NOT MY MOM!

For a teenage boy:
FIRE! FIRE! HE'S NOT MY BROTHER!

For a teenage girl:
FIRE! FIRE! SHE'S NOT MY SISTER!

There are very real reasons for this scenario and specific techniques.

First, this type of yell, looking and pointing technique is different from when Mom or Dad take a child home. We all have seen a child scream and cry when Mom or Dad have cut their play time off at the park. When it's time to go home a lot of kids will throw tantrums or fuss.

Fussing or tantrums do not look like **FIRE! FIRE! HE'S NOT MY DAD!** Fussing or tantrums do not have abdominal yells, direct eye contact and pointing at anyone holding on to a child.

So, we make the yell different, noticeable and very effective.

Second, we teach the child to perform this yell sequence until they get help. It's more than a one time thing. It's a continual sequence of events and movements.

In the event the child is not helped or let go, we equip them to escape and run for help with our **9 Easy GETAWAYS**.

9 Easy Getaways

Here are the Keeping Kids Safe **9 Easy GETAWAYS**. We teach them to all our classes. They are effective and can be done by even the smallest and youngest child of four.

- **Inside Up**

- **Inside Down**

- **Outside Up**

- **Outside Down**

- **Two Hand Grab**

- **Thumb In The Front**

- **Thumb In The Back**

- **Neck Choke**

- **Pick Up**

The **9 Easy GETAWAYS** cover a complete range of possibilities on how a child could be grabbed. They even cover being grabbed by someone who sneaks up on the child.

Each technique is specific in its application. Each technique is simple and easy for any child to remember and execute. In teaching these in the classroom, we take great care in making sure each child executes each technique correctly so they learn them in their most effective manner.

We introduce these **9 Easy GETAWAYS** three at a time in our classes. Some are similar in body position and application so grouping them accelerates learning for the kids. Parents, and as large as we can find, act as grabbers and each child learns to execute each escape technique properly.

We encourage families to practice these 9 Easy GETAWAYS at home. To reinforce this we give a small handout for parents to place on their refrigerator doors that remind them of each **9 Easy GETAWAYS.** Once a child learns a **9 Easy GETAWAY** these small reminders help easily along with home practice sessions.

- **Inside Up**
  Clasp hands under chin – elbows together – spin

- **Inside Down**
  Hand in front of belly – straight arm – step up & zoom away

- **Outside Up**
  Reach under the hand – grab – make a "U"

- **Outside Down**
  Reach over the arm – bend elbows – bring hands to shoulders

- **Two Hand Grab**
  Reach between the arms – bend elbows – bring hands to shoulders

- **Thumb In The Front**
  BIG circle backwards over arm – punch

- **Thumb In The Back**
  TWO BIG circles forward

- **Neck Choke**
  Lift arms straight over head – place arms on ears – spin

- **Pick Up**
  Wiggle the hips

Chapter Summary

- Teach your child to project and be confident.

- Teach your child to move quickly and steadily.

- Teach your child to stand up with their head up, eyes alert and back straight.

- Teach your child to listen to their Belly Brain.

- Teach your child to engage a Circle of Safety and command "STOP! I'm not suppose to get close to Strangers!" if a stranger gets too close to them.

- Teach your child to turn and run and yell "FIRE!" when a bad stranger invades their Circle Of Safety.

- Teach your child to find a police officer, fire fighter or Mother with other children if they ever get separated from you in a shopping mall or store.

Keeping Kids Safe
9 Easy Getaways

- **Inside Up**
  Clasp hands under chin – elbows together – spin

- **Inside Down**
  Hand in front of belly – straight arm – step up & swing away

- **Outside Up**
  Reach under the hand – grab – make a U

- **Outside Down**
  Reach over the arm – bend elbows – bring hands to shoulders

- **Two Hand Grab**
  Reach over the arm – bend elbows – bring hands to shoulders

- **Thumb In The Front**
  BIG circle backwards over arm –
  punch

- **Thumb In The Back**
  TWO BIG circles forward

- **Neck Choke**
  Lift arms straight over head – place
  arms on ears – spin

- **Pick Up**
  Wiggle the hips

10

ABOUT THE AUTHORS

The Riches Of A Single Thought

A single thought is powerful. A single thought produces riches beyond imagination. Keeping Kids Safe started with a single thought.

Amazing things happen, riches for all, by following that single thought with action. Keeping Kids Safe started over twenty years ago on a single thought.

Preston Jones is the creator and developer of Keeping Kids Safe. The program began as a labor of love intended to make a positive difference in the lives of children and their families. It started by agreeing to help a single family be safer following an idea, a single thought.

Today, Keeping Kids Safe is a culmination of thirty years of experience, expertise and constant dedication by Preston Jones. He is continually evaluating and improving the program as the world we live in changes. His ultimate goal is to offer every child the opportunity to grow up feeling safe and secure and confident in themselves.

Preston Jones honed his approach to child safety through a prolific thirty year career focusing on personal safety for a variety of age groups and organizations. From Keeping Kids Safe to police and security departments, his expertise has helped thousands learn to keep themselves safe.

His devotion to the subject of child safety and kids being given the chance to be the best they can be, stems from being a father of daughters and a former police officer, Air Force veteran, Martial Arts Fifth Degree Black Belt, and university student studying psychology and parapsychology.

Preston started developing self-defense programs for the general public in 1976. He developed his own ideas on children's personal safety and created programs from these ideas and his own personal observations and experiments.

Eight years later, the power of a single thought, he agreed to provide martial art and focus training to a family with a teenage son who had a behavioral disorder. A single, rich thought, helped Preston realized the need for a program on personal safety for kids.

The actual development of a safety program for elementary age children followed which he constantly improved, evolved and updated. Today's Keeping Kids Safe program is current, modern and effective in today's world. It is state-of-the-art for kid's safety.

Preston's expertise goes further than this. In 1991, he was approached by the City of Walnut Creek, California to begin an adaptive martial arts program for children and adults with special needs. In 1996 the position of program coordinator in the City of Walnut Creek's Specialized Recreation Department became vacant and he stepped in to fill it when asked to do so.

Since taking over the program, Preston, and the Department, has received numerous awards from both the City of Walnut Creek and the Developmental Disabilities Council of Contra Costa and Alameda counties. The highly praised program continues today.

Preston's programs and seminars are sought out by public and private schools and agencies such as Boys and Girl Scouts of America, Highlands Hospital in Oakland, CA, De Young Museum in San Francisco, CA, and a variety of different security agencies throughout the San Francisco bay area. His expertise extends to include defensive tactics, baton training, handcuffing techniques, and small arms firearm training, which he has presented to both police officers and private security guards.

Joyce Jackson is also a part of Keeping Kids Safe.

She came across Preston Jones and Keeping Kids Safe when her oldest son was 4 years old. As a parent, she constantly worried about her child's safety in today's disturbing world. With a single thought followed up with action, she enrolled her son in Keeping Kids Safe.

Joyce's personal evolution into an instrumental role with Keeping Kids Safe, coupled with a tenacious persistence to keep as many kids as possible safe and secure, has catapulted her into the forefront of child safety with Preston.

Keeping Kids Safe continues to empower children to be the best they can be. If kids can walk down the street with their shoulders back, head held high, eyes bright and aware of the environment, they are less of a target for predators.

Keeping Kids Safe is about safe kids and better families. Preston and Joyce, along with their program, make a difference in people's lives. They do it in their unique approach that folds the parent into the process of teaching their child to keep themselves safer.

It all started with Preston Jones. You can now be a welcomed member of the Keeping Kids Safe family. It is timely, effective, so simple and filled with common sense and here to help you and your child.

Preston and Joyce will help you to mentor to your kids. It will enable you to keep them safer today than yesterday. By being a Keeping Kids Safe family member and living the principles of teaching your kids to keep themselves safe, you teach them safety principles for a lifetime. The precept of "Don't Give Them A Fish, Teach Them How To Fish" is what Keeping Kids Safe is all about.

Revealing The Secrets Behind The Keeping Kids Safe Program

Keeping Kids Safe is about safe kids, safe families. It works best and most effectively when parents embrace the concepts as an adult and bring it to their entire family. In short, it's a way of life.

For the last twenty years we have been developing and teaching the Keeping Kids Safe program. We have found unequivocally that if you focus on the kids, then focus on the parents, get them both to buy into being the best human beings they can be, then and only then can we teach them real, effective and life long safety techniques. We know if we do not follow this sequence, the safety of the child, by virtue of them being able to keep themselves safe, is always in question.

Our program has got to be about kids being able to keep themselves safe. Every child is safe when Mom or Dad is around. It is all about kids who find themselves alone and without Mom and Dad for any reason.

Our extensive backgrounds in psychology, personal safety, martial arts and community based teaching programs has allowed us to combine a number of areas of expertise into one very effective series of safety classes. We even have specialty safety classes that cover a range of age groups.

While the main focus of what we do is for elementary age children, we have programs that work with expectant Moms through toddler age children, teen programs, and safety programs for college co-eds. There is also a Special Needs Recreational program that is very close to our hearts, too.

In Walnut Creek, California we "home base" with our basic series of ten classes, once a week, throughout the year. Each class in the series runs 45 minutes a session.

The basic course outline looks like this for the kids:

- Introduction
    - 2 Keeping Kids Safe Rules
- Be Like A Super Hero
    - Be The Best You Can Be
- Move Like A Super Hero
    - Fast and Quick
    - Stand and Sit With ZOOM!
- Super Hero Focus Powers
- Super Hero Laser Eyes
- Super Hero Power Voice
- Keeping Kids Safe 9 Easy Getaways

For the parents, our course covers:

- Self Confidence
- Mental Focus
- Communication
- Empowering Your Child

- Power of Real Observation
- Having Fun With Your Kid
- Keeping Kids Safe 9 Easy Getaways

Some of what we teach you may know. It is our "approach" to safety that is unique. A lot of what we teach you may not know. We will change that.

A good part of our philosophy of safety is controversial. To that we say "good!" We want to work with parents and kids that completely buy into our philosophy. We tell parents in the first class that we are going to say things they may not agree with. We are going to say things that will make them uncomfortable. We are going to say things in which they may disagree with us.

Many parents in our classes like what they hear and some do not. We are very clear and up front with our ideas on keeping kids safe. If a parent is not committed 100% to our program it will not work for them or their child. They are wasting their time.

The first thing we tell parents is that they are responsible for their child's safety. We tell them real safety begins at home. We tell them real safety is also reinforced at home by Mom and Dad. We tell parents directly that they have to be the best they can be in order to teach their kids to be the best they can be.

Talking to the parents is how we start but we relate directly to the kids, too. For example, we make everything we teach exciting and fun for the kids, even with a serious subject like safety.

We've designed it that way. It's part of our "Simplicity By Design" philosophy to safety. We know how to teach kids. We teach in a way that makes each class fun for them in a number of carefully crafted ways. One way is by using language they use. We engage the children and let them tell us what they think about a number of subjects we broach. In doing so we listen carefully to their words. In responding we use the exact same words the children use since they understand what those words mean. We also use the words in the same manner the kids do. Using the same words in the same way enables us to connect with the kids almost instantly.

We also sequence information in ways we know kids will absorb it and retain it. We know how to teach kids so they learn effectively and quickly.

We introduce certain concepts and terms in the first few weeks to both parents and kids. We subtly weave concepts together with a series of exercises and games that aid and reinforce the learning process within the kids.

While we teach the children themselves we work with the families as a total unit. Whatever we work on needs to be reinforced and practiced at home. This includes the confidence building and mental focus building techniques. This is why we say we have a secondary focus that is to make families better by learning and practicing safety together.

Kids need the security and companionship of a group, of a "unit." We believe this unit should be a family, a solid, positive, nurturing family.

We simply accent the family for greater child safety.

11

APPENDIX

Keeping Kids Safe Games To Play At Home

This book is about HOW to protect your kids from sexual predators. The easiest "HOW" is in playing games with your child that subtly teaches them our safety techniques.

Games are the best way to teach your child real safety for a lifetime because it teaches them in ways they can understand. Games teach your child in a fun manner that is exciting.

Again, kids love games and more than that, they love to play them. So, here are some of our ideas for great games at home with your child that teaches them our safety techniques.

Basically, any game you play with your child that engages and expands their awareness of their environment and focus abilities will keep them safer when you are not around.

Remember, the secret to successfully engaging your child in any game is:

1. Get their attention
    a. No distractions
    b. Eye contact

2. Get their buy-in to the game
    a. Engage them in conversation in their terms

3. Give them a "win" reward for playing it well

4. Make it fun and exciting

Also, have fun yourself with them and make up your own games. Be creative and enjoy the time spent with your child.

Keeping Kids Safe Focus Games

The Shopping Game

In this game, give your child a fun place to
go shopping, like the toy store or pet shop.
Give them a list of four or five thing they are
going to shop for and have them repeat the
list back to you.

The key here is to have your child excited
about where they get to shop. Let them pick
a place. Make it their choice. It immediately
gets them to "buy into" the game.

Second, make sure you have their complete
attention. Keep the duration of the games,
short, fun and exciting. The game goes
something like this:

DAD: Mike, want to play a game?

MIKE: OK!

DAD: Let's play the shopping game. Where
would you like to go?

MIKE: The toy store!

DAD: Great! Now, I'm going to give you a
list of five things to get at the toy store.
Look right at your shoes. Ready?

MIKE: Yes!

DAD: You're going to the toy store and
you're going to get a ball, toy truck, hula
hoop, video game and a small stuffed dog.

DAD: Now, Mike, tell me what you are going to get.

MIKE: Uh….a ball, toy truck, a …uh…hula hoop, hmmm.

DAD: OK, now Mike. Look me right in the eyes. You're going to the toy store and you're going to get a blue bike, a doll, a toy soldier, a ball and a green turtle. Now, look me in the eyes and tell me what you are going to get.

MIKE: A blue bike, a doll, a toy soldier, a ball and a green turtle.

DAD: Great Job! You're super!

Simple, but this game works time and again just like this scenario above.

All of the games we suggest are similar in format. Get your child's attention, get them to buy into the game, make it exciting, fun and play!

The Grocery Store Game
This game can be played when you go to the grocery store with your child. You can announce the game before heading into store and have your child keep on the lookout for yellow vegetables, boxes of cereal that are orange or green bottles of soda.

You can also ask them afterwards what the checkout clerk looked like. Tune into physical characteristics and clothing as you ask your child questions.

At The Drive Thru Game
Quiz your child about what they saw when you went through the Drive Thru at your favorite fast food restaurant.

The Gas Station Game
Play this game of observation with your child when you fill up your car.

The Who Blinks First Game
This silly little game is one we all grew up playing but it teaches focus powers exceptionally well. Play staring contests with your child and challenge them to longer and longer periods of staring.

The Who Can Sit Still The Longest Game
This popular game is another we all grew up playing. You can do this even during the commercial breaks of your child's favorite TV shows.

The Stand Up! Sit Down! Game
This is a fun game that is popular at birthday parties for prizes but you can do it any time with your child. It's especially effective if you have more than one child and offer a "win" prize at the end.

The Changing Things Game

This fun game is played by having your child look around a specific room, having them leave the room and rearranging a few items in the room. Then call them back in the room and see what has been moved.

Bulk Orders

Groups, Organizations, Companies and Corporations

Keeping Kids Safe offers Bulk Order book discounts

For Information Go To
http://pycbookbulk.com

Safety For A Lifetime

Keeping Kids Safe

FREE Bi Monthly Ezine

One of the **TOP** Child Safety Ezines on the Internet today!

Packed with tips, strategies, information and help keeping your child safe in today's dangerous world.

Subscribe At